access to politics

LOCAL *and* REGIONAL GOVERNMENT *in* BRITAIN

Neil McNaughton

Series Editor: David Simpson

Hodder & Stoughton

A MEMBER OF THE HODDER HEADLINE GROUP

ACKNOWLEDGEMENTS

The publishers would like to thank the following for granting permission to use photos:

Jon Blau/Camera Press London: page 20
Topham Picture Source: page 35
Press Association/Topham: page 60
David Toose/Travel Ink: page 105

Order queries: please contact Bookpoint Ltd, 130 Milton Park, Abingdon, Oxon OX14 4SB. Telephone: (44) 01235 400414. Fax: (44) 01235 400454. Lines are open from 9.00–6.00, Monday to Saturday, with a 24-hour message answering service. Email address: orders@bookpoint.co.uk

A catalogue record for this title is available from The British Library

ISBN 0 340 711841

First published 1998
Impression number 10   9   8   7   6   5   4   3
Year   2002   2001

Cover photo of Manchester Town Hall from: Jan Chlebik

Typeset by Transet Limited, Coventry, England.
Printed in Great Britain for Hodder & Stoughton Educational, a division of Hodder Headline plc, 338 Euston Road, London NW1 3BH by The Bath Press, Bath

CONTENTS

PREFACE

A/AS Level syllabuses in Government and Politics aim to develop knowledge and understanding of the political system of the UK. They cover its local, national and European Union dimensions, and include comparative studies of aspects of other political systems, in order to ensure an understanding of the distinctive nature of the British political system. The minimum requirements for comparative study are aspects of systems with a separation of powers, how other systems protect the rights of individuals and how other electoral systems work.

Access to Politics is a series of concise topic books which cover the syllabus requirements, providing students with the necessary resources to complete the course successfully.

General advice on approaching exam questions

To achieve high grades you need to demonstrate consistency. Clearly address all parts of a question, make good use of essay plans or notes, and plan your time to cover all the questions.

Make your answers stand out from the crowd by using contemporary material to illustrate them. You should read a quality newspaper and listen to or watch appropriate programmes on radio and television.

Skills Advice

You should comprehend, synthesise and interpret political information in a variety of forms:

- Analyse and evaluate political institutions, processes and behaviour, political arguments and explanations.
- Identify parallels, connections, similarities and differences between aspects of the political systems studied.
- Select and organise relevant material to construct arguments and explanations leading to reasoned conclusions.
- Communicate the arguments with relevance, clarity and coherence, using vocabulary appropriate to the study of Government and Politics.

David Simpson

1

INTRODUCTION

FROM TIME TO time, the attention of the public is drawn to local political affairs by the printed and broadcast media. Occasionally, the tabloid press carries a story of scandal or corruption at a town hall. The 1980s, certainly, were punctuated by news of the latest antics of so-called 'loony left' Labour councillors who were spending taxpayers' money on what were seen as 'wasteful' projects involving the unemployed, young offenders, single parents and a variety of apparently 'marginal' members of society. The more serious broadsheets have also highlighted periodic bouts of conflict between government ministers and stubborn councils who wished to spend more money than central government wished them to do.

In the 1990s, attention switched to Conservative councils; they were attempting to swim against the tide of opinion which regarded them as the lapdogs of the government, desperate to hold onto power at a time when their party was steadily losing ground to a revitalised Labour Party. Each set of local election results signalled new losses for the Conservatives until, by 1996, it was difficult to find a Conservative-controlled council anywhere in the country. The story of gerrymandering in Westminster council in London was given much media attention; it came to light that it was moving poorer families out of its housing stock and into other boroughs, and replacing them with better-off tenants. The purpose was to increase the proportion of likely Conservative voters at a time when there was a possibility of the party losing control of the borough's council.

But such tales have merely pandered to the prurient curiosity of the electorate rather than their genuine interest in local government affairs. In truth, lack of interest in or knowledge of local government is widespread in Britain. The apparent obsession of the media with national politics inevitably crowds out news from the regions – except for the kind of story described above.

An extremely vigorous local press has developed particularly since the advent of 'free' newspapers. These are a welcome addition to a pluralist democracy which thrives on the dissemination of political information. But there remains a deep-seated apathy where local government is concerned. There is little of the lively participative enthusiasm of Americans for community politics in Britain. Few people here can name any of their local councillors; they are unlikely to know which party or parties controls the council; and many will not be aware of which services are the responsibility of their local council and which are controlled by central government or one of its **quangos** or agencies.

A vivid illustration of such indifference occurred in 1981, when Michael Heseltine MP was Secretary of State for the Environment, and thus responsible for local government. He ordered a trial referendum in Coventry to determine whether the community would accept a substantial rise in local taxation. Only 25 per cent of the relevant electorate bothered to vote and the experiment had to be abandoned.

WHY STUDY LOCAL AND REGIONAL GOVERNMENT?

Why should you be concerned with local or regional politics when they are of little interest to most of the population? The answer is that, despite public ignorance and apathy, levels of government below the centre remain a key part of our political system. There are a number of justifications for this interest:

- A large proportion of public expenditure is accounted for by local and regional bodies.
- Significantly large numbers of people are employed directly by local and regional bodies, or by their agents.
- A significant number of key services are partially or completely controlled by these institutions. Among them are education, low-cost housing, policing, refuse collection and disposal, libraries, parks and gardens, the planning of roads, housing and commercial development, environmental protection, public and individual health care, family social services, emergency services, consumer protection.
- There are now proposals for large transfers of power from central government to new regional institutions. These transfers are likely to have significant political, financial and cultural effects on many communities.
- The ongoing process of restructuring local government is altering everyday life of smaller communities.
- There are plans for fundamental changes in the relationship between the national minorities in the British Isles – Scots, Welsh and Ulster people.
- The structure of Europe is also undergoing change. These developments will inevitably impinge upon the distribution of power within Britain.

In short, few political factors are likely to have such deep-seated effects on the political system as developments in local and regional government. Vital changes have already taken place in the last quarter of the twentieth century, and, in the last few years of the century, a large swathe of crucial proposals for change are to be debated. The political map of Britain may be dramatically altered as we enter the new millennium.

The election of a Labour government on 1 May 1997 signalled the potential for major changes in Britain's political agenda. Not least among these developments stands the prospect of significant shifts in the distribution of power in the political system. Some of these changes are likely to occur *within* central government, eg alterations in the composition and powers of the House of Lords; changes in the relationship between government and Parliament or between ministers and the administration which they control. It is certainly true, however, that changes in the powers and functions of the various *levels* of government will have the most important consequences.

Five levels or *layers* of government affecting Britain can be identified. These are, in descending order of scale:

1　global international organisations such as NATO or the United Nations
2　the European Union (EU)
3　national government
4　regional government
5　local government

It is beyond the scope of this book to consider the first level, global organisations. Nor are we directly concerned with Europe here, though it must always be borne in mind that the activities of the EU affect all three layers of government below it. Indeed, today's student of any aspect of British government must always ask whether Europe does or will have some influence on the way in which institutions and political processes operate. The circumstances in which the EU does become relevant will be identified as they arise in this text, but this area will not be covered separately.

The way in which power is divided between the three lowest levels, national, regional and local, is the main concern of this work. There are three essential questions to be asked about these aspects of government:

- What is the territorial jurisdiction of each level? The term 'national' is fairly straight forward, but to differentiate between 'regional' and 'local' is less simple.
- What powers and responsibilities does each level possess and what are the prospects for future developments?
- What is the nature of the relationship between each level? What controls exist? Who raises the money? How are joint decisions made?

QUESTIONS AND CASE STUDIES

LOCAL GOVERNMENT QUESTIONS

The majority of questions which are asked of politics students concern the following:

- How have the powers, functions and responsibilities of local government changed in modern times?
- How has the relationship between local and central (and perhaps regional) government developed in recent years?
- What has been the relationship between financial arrangements and the broader role or operation of local government?
- What is the current state of local government 'democracy'?
- What are the prospects for future change?

Of course other, more specialised questions may be posed, especially on degree courses, but to be successful, you should generally be prepared to cover these issues.

REGIONAL GOVERNMENT QUESTIONS

By the nature of the subject, these issues tend to be speculative, but answers cannot be vague:

- What arguments can be marshalled in favour of, and against, the extension of regional government in Britain as a whole?
- Similar questions arise which are related specifically to devolution of power specifically to England, Scotland, Wales and Northern Ireland.
- In what senses has the development of the EU influenced the debate over the future of regional government?
- What kinds of democratic institutions will be required if regional government is to be successfully extended in Britain?

CASE STUDIES

Local government abounds with suitable topics for case studies and coursework assignments. The more interesting include housing, education, public transport, environmental protection and enhancement, and planning. Each field of responsibility which local authorities are expected to undertake is different, so that it is a mistake to assume that the same approach can be adopted in any subject of study. Nevertheless, you may find it useful if the following factors are considered in any extended study.

- What is the nature of the legislation which governs the responsibilities and services in question?

- What are the financial arrangements for funding the activity or, where applicable, for charging for services?
- To what extent and in what ways do central government and its ministers or officials control the activity?
- What arrangements are made by the local authority itself in order to carry out its responsibilities?
- What other bodies may be concerned? These may include quangos, central government agencies, voluntary organisations or charities, private enterprises or other financial institutions.
- Which pressure groups may be involved? Are they 'insiders' or 'outsiders'?

Suitably armed with these essential details, you may then extend the assignment to meet the specific demands of the question which is to be addressed. This book, together with the recommended further reading, is designed to explain these key aspects of local government.

FIRST PRINCIPLES

Before going any further there are a number of basic terms and meanings which must be understood. There is a glossary of key terms at the end of this book, but the following principles require a fuller explanation:

- tiering
- subsidiarity
- democracy
- devolution
- regional government
- federalism
- the unitary state.

TIERING

Local government is arranged in a series of levels which are normally referred to as **tiers**. The whole of Britain is divided into administrative areas, the largest of which we describe as 'first tier'. Each of these large units may then be further split into smaller units – the second tier authorities. In some parts of the country there is also a very small scale third tier, but this is largely confined to rural areas.

As we shall see in the next chapter, there is no common system of tiering in Britain despite a number of past attempts to rationalise the structure. Furthermore, if and when regional government is introduced, there will be a further tier added in all or part of the country.

To illustrate, the arrangements for Hertfordshire which includes all three tiers, are shown on page 6.

Layers of council
County
Borough
District
Parish
North Hertfordshire
Stevenage
East Hertfordshire
Dacorum
St Albans
Welwyn Hatfield
Broxbourne
Hertsmere
Watford
Three Rivers

THREE TIERS OF LOCAL GOVERNMENT IN HERTFORDSHIRE

SUBSIDIARITY

This principle has long been a cornerstorne of the constitutional policies of the Liberal Democrat Party. It gained further credibility when it was enshrined as one of the basic principles of the Maastricht Treaty of the European Union which was agreed in 1992. By the time of its election to office in 1997, the Labour Party had also given it tentative support.

In essence, **subsidiarity** means that:

> *government should be provided at the smallest (ie, most local) level possible which is consistent with the efficient and acceptable delivery of services.*

For example, it is clear that the security of the country as a whole in terms of external defence must be provided either at *national* or *European* level. Smaller scale communities would be simply unable to finance and organise the sophisticated modern weaponry required today. When we consider such services as housing or social services, however, there is clearly a choice. If subsidiarity is applied these will be pushed down to the most local level, but only if a satisfactory standard can be maintained.

Article A of the Common provisions of the Treaty on European Union (Maastricht) of 1992 includes the following statement:

> *This Treaty marks a new stage in the process of creating an even closer union among the peoples of Europe, in which decisions are taken as closely as possible to the citizen.*

The reason for the adoption of the idea is to maximise democratic control, as it is assumed that small scale government is more subject to public choice, control and accountability than if it were organised on a larger scale. However, as we shall see, governments who have an overwhelming desire to reduce public expenditure are under constant pressure to *increase* the scale of local government in order to reap the benefits of economic efficiency (what economists call **economies of scale**).

Table 1 suggests a *possible* scheme of government, showing examples of how services could be divided between different levels or tiers on the basis of subsidiarity. Where a service appears on more than one level, it may be a shared function.

Table 1: *A possible scheme of government*					
FUNCTION	LEVEL OF GOVERNMENT				
	EUROPE	NATION	REGION	UPPER TIER LOCAL	LOWER TIER LOCAL
External defence	X	X			
Road transport	X	X	X	X	
Primary education			X	X	X
Low cost housing				X	
Care of the elderly					X

DEMOCRACY

It is very easy to talk glibly of 'democracy' in the context of local or regional government, but it does need to be defined more specifically than is often the case. For the purposes of this book, therefore, we shall include the following elements in any judgement of whether democracy is being served:

- Are people, as individuals or in groups, able to influence decision-making?
- Are there opportunities for individuals or groups to have their grievances heard and, where appropriate, redressed? For example, the removal of nuisance of hazards or the establishment of fair treatment in housing, social care and planning decisions.

- Do individuals have opportunities to participate in political processes, independently, through parties or in pressure groups?
- Are people informed of how and why decisions are being made, and of what the main local and regional issues are?
- Does that level of government make itself properly accountable to the people and/or to their elected representatives?

Though we may be able to suggest or discover further democratic principles, we will adopt those described above as a 'working definition'. It now becomes clearer how the issues of scale and democracy relate to one another. This is a recurring theme in local and regional government.

DEVOLUTION

There may be a problem in distinguishing between the terms 'devolution' and 'regional government'. In truth there is no fixed distinction. For our purposes, however, we will define devolution as:

---

the establishment of autonomous government in regions which consider themselves to have a national identity, but without transferring legal sovereignty to such national regions.

There are three basic forms of devolution:

1 **Legislative:** The power to make laws relating to the region.
2 **Administrative:** The responsibility for the execution of laws within a region, including financial expenditure.
3 **Financial:** The power to exercise all or some control over the raising of revenue within the region. In particular, this relates to the power to raise taxes or to vary the level of taxation.

So, when we speak of devolution, we need to be clear about which of the three types described above we are referring to. Proposals for devolution may, in practice, relate to all three or only one or two of them.

REGIONAL GOVERNMENT

We can define this in the same way as we have described 'devolution' above. The difference is that a 'region' may not have a *national* identity. Thus, Scotland is a national region, whereas the North West of England may be described simply as an *administrative* region. Lest Lancastrians or Cumbrians object to this bland description, it should be stressed that this does not preclude the idea that a region such as the North-West does have its own separate *cultural* identity. But 'culture' is not the same as 'nation'!

So regional government refers to the idea of splitting a country – England in this case – into large areas to which power may be devolved as shown above. Naturally, since the regional identity of such areas will probably be weaker than the nationalistic feelings in Wales, Scotland and Northern Ireland, there is likely to be a reduced demand for devolution of power to them.

FEDERALISM

In the debates over further European integration which have reached a crescendo in the 1990s, federalism has become flippantly known by its opponents as the 'f-word'. At first sight this seems to be over-reaction as it is not immediately distinguishable from national or regional devolution. This is a mistake. There is a crucial and fundamental difference which must be understood.

In a federal state **legal sovereignty** and not merely political power is transferred to a region. This means that those transferred powers are described and entrenched (safeguarded) in a constitution. In this way they cannot be removed or overruled by the central government or legislature, unless the constitution itself is amended. The proposals for devolution or regional government do not include plans for transfer of sovereignty. Thus, Parliament in London would remain sovereign and so be able to take back its former powers or, in defined circumstances, overrule decisions made in a region.

Many large states, including Germany, the USA and Russia, have federal systems. Their regions (known as *laender*, states and republics respectively) have their own sovereign powers which are reserved to them. Spain, on the other hand, has adopted a regional system (regions are known there as *autonomies*). The government in Madrid retains overall sovereign control.

THE UNITARY STATE

This is effectively the converse of a federal system. Here all legal sovereignty is reserved to central government and/or parliament. Any powers transferred are, thus, only *delegated* and so can be returned to the centre as long as proper legal procedures are followed.

Clearly Britain is a **unitary state** and there is no realistic prospect of its reverting to federalism (though some kind of federal arrangement with Northern Ireland in the future remains a possibility). Even the Scottish and Welsh National Parties have not proposed a federal solution. Their position remains that the two alternatives are devolution or complete independence, but not federalism.

STUDY   GUIDE

Practice Questions

1 Distinguish between
  a   subsidiarity
  b   devolution
  c   federalism
2 **a**   What is meant by the term subsidiarity?
  b   Why is it an important principle of the European Union?

2

THE STRUCTURE OF LOCAL GOVERNMENT IN BRITAIN

Introduction

THIS CHAPTER WILL detail the developments which have taken place in recent years in the structure of local government in England, Wales, Scotland and Northern Ireland.

'Structure' means two things for local government:

- where the boundaries lie between different local authority areas, including how local government areas are divided up into smaller units where they are so divided; and
- how the functions and responsibilities of local government are allocated to these units.

In considering structure, we will describe the reasons why local development has developed as it has and what are the consequences of those arrangements.

Key Points

This chapter contains material on the following key issues:

- Why the scale of local authorities is important. This includes the nature of the relationship between the size of a local authority and questions of efficiency and democracy.
- The development of local government structure since the 1970s, why changes were made and what were their effects.
- The work of the Local Government Commission in England and equivalent bodies in Scotland and Northern Ireland.

- How structure may change in the future, in particular the possible restoration of an authority for the whole of London.

BASIC PRINCIPLES

Before considering the nature and development of how local government is structured, there are some fundamental issues which should be taken into account. They can be reduced to three elements:

- culture and tradition
- efficiency
- democracy.

CULTURE AND TRADITION

It is important not to lose sight of the fact that many people feel a close emotional attachment to the place where they live and have grown up. Despite the apathy about local political affairs, which we have described above, such affinities do result in concern about the institutions which are connected with 'place'.

Furthermore, many British locations have a well known and significant history, sometimes stretching back to Roman time (ie, 2,000 years) and very often to the Norman conquest in 1066. Such towns and cities as York, Edinburgh, Colchester, Londonderry, Cardiff and Winchester have a rich heritage of which their inhabitants are proud. If alterations to political boundaries and institutions threaten their specific identity, their communities will become understandably uneasy.

Some cities have found a new character, born of relatively recent changes. Liverpool's role in modern entertainment, Manchester's and Newcastle's association with football (as well as Liverpool again, of course!), London's international importance and the close association between Edinburgh or Glasgow and the Arts have all created a new sense of the importance of locality.

Counties, too, carry strong popular allegiances. There is no historical logic to the development of British counties so that the patchwork pattern which we see on any political map has simply grown up through a series of events and accidents some of which can be traced deep into history. But attachments to one's county, especially in rural areas are important. Yorkshire, Cornwall and Kent are clear examples of this phenomenon. In addition, a number of sports are still organised on the basis of county. Cricket is the most important illustration, but the same is true of amateur levels of football, tennis, golf and rugby. We should not under-estimate the strength of such regional loyalties.

EFFICIENCY

There is a general assumption that, the larger an organisation is, the more efficiently it can use the resources available to it. In broad terms this is true. Clearly the costs of bureaucracy can be spread more effectively in a large political body. Big authorities can enjoy the benefits of bulk purchasing of resources, can use their manpower more rationally and will have substantial funds available for large scale projects. There are also some responsibilities which must inevitably be undertaken on a large scale. These include road planning, public transport and economic development.

So there are indeed pressures to keep political units as large as possible in the interests of cost saving. However, important developments in the way in which services are organised may challenge these assumptions. Increasingly, as we shall see below, local authorities are being forced or encouraged to 'buy in' services from private companies or voluntary organisations. This may enable smaller government units to enjoy the benefits of the greater efficiency of these larger organisations.

Take refuse collection, for example. A small, lower tier authority, may find it extremely expensive to organise a small operation which requires high levels of investment in plant and machinery. But if that authority purchases the service from a large, privately run, national company, it can enjoy economies of scale even after the private firm has taken its necessary profit. A similar analysis could be applied to such operations as parks and gardens maintenance, house building and repairs or environmental protection. A theoretical example may clarify this principle: see table 2, which shows that it may be possible for a small authority to provide a service as cheaply as a larger one, if it can use an efficient private firm.

Table 2: *Refuse collection service*			
PROVIDER	NO. OF HOUSEHOLDS	TOTAL COST (ANNUAL)	COST PER HOUSEHOLD
Large authority	500,000	£40,000,000	£80
Small authority	10,000	£1,000,000	£100
Private company	10,000	£800,000	£80

Alternatively, it is feasible that a number of neighbouring authorities can cooperate in organising large scale services. Thus the authorities can remain small, but still share in the control of major responsibilities. Although this is a common practice in the United States and continental Europe, there are few examples in Britain. One exception, however, was the Inner London Education Authority (ILEA). This was a cooperation among 12 inner London boroughs to provide education in an area which shared common problems resulting from poverty and social problems. From 1965–1990, it proved partially successful in overcoming the special difficulties of inner London, but eventually fell foul of Margaret Thatcher's opposition to large scale local government.

DEMOCRACY

Just as greater size is assumed to bring efficiency, so smallness is usually thought to promote greater democracy. The reasoning is that in small communities there are more opportunities for people to influence decision-makers and to involve themselves in political activity. It is also true that more information about the local authorities' work is likely to be absorbed by the electorate.

In so far as democracy also means choice (about the quantity, variety and nature of services provided), it must be true that the larger the number of local authorities which exist, the more diversity there will be. Broad scale authorities must inevitably mean uniformity over large geographical authorities.

There may be no actual proof that 'small is beautiful' in democratic terms, but it is certainly perceived to be preferable by those who hold broadly liberal beliefs.

SYNTHESIS OF PRINCIPLES

Policy-makers in this field thus face great difficulty in trying to reconcile three principles which are, to some extent, conflicting. It is not possible to satisfy the needs for retaining traditional community identities, promoting maximum efficiency and retaining democratic institutions with one system and structure. It will come as no surprise, therefore, to find that the recent history of attempts to create a permanent, rational structure for local government, lacks a sense of coherence.

STRUCTURAL CHANGE

Adding to the problems described above, efforts to re-organise local government in Britain have suffered from political discontinuity. Any change of this kind must, by its nature, take several years to implement. Redrawing lines on a map might seem to be simple, but the arrangements for consultation, the transferring of service provision, financial adjustments, and necessary legislation form a complex operation. So restructuring is likely to be handled by more than one minister and often by governments controlled by a different party.

The **Redcliffe-Maud** proposals which are described on p 21, are a perfect example. Appointed by a Labour government in the 1960s, this committee reported to a new Conservative administration in 1970; the legislation was passed in 1972, but final implementation was delayed until 1974 when Labour had regained power. In the course of this procedure at least four different ministers were responsible for the reorganisation! Small wonder, therefore, that the result was a series of compromises and the new structure only lasted for 12 years.

Fortunately the picture is considerably simpler in Northern Ireland, Scotland and Wales. The cause of this simplicity lies in the fact that changes have been largely left in the hands of permanent civil servants, with relatively little political interference.

SCOTLAND

There have been two modern stages of development. In 1974 the recommendations of the **Wheatley Committee** were implemented, creating a two tier system for most of the country. This is shown in table 3.

Table 3: *Scottish local government 1974–96*			
TIER	TYPE	NUMBER	FUNCTIONS (EXAMPLES)
First	Regions	9	Education, policing
Second	Districts	53	Social services, care of the elderly
Unitary	Islands	3	Most services

The special features of this system included:

- Great variation in the size of the nine regions. This was the inevitable result of the particular geographical features of Scotland, with densely populated areas punctuating large areas with sparse populations.
- For the same reasons, the districts also varied considerably in size.
- The Island regions (Shetland, Orkney and the Western Isles) have their own geographical problems and so could not be split in the same way. They were 'unitary' authorities with most functions of both tiers.
- Communities were given the option of setting up their own **community councils** for self government on a very small (mostly village) scale. These had very few minor responsibilities, such as local traffic management, but even so, over 1,300 were set up as a result of local choice.

The second stage took place in the 1990s and was implemented in 1996 (though the councils were elected one year before). The system was a simple one – 28 unitary authorities were established, replacing the former two tier system. The old community councils were retained, but in principle this was a single system.

The need to ensure that authorities have some traditional and economic coherence, means that the size of the new authorities varies a great deal. So 'City of Glasgow', the largest, contains over 600,000 people, while the smallest (though not geographically) is 'Orkney and Shetland' at about 20,000 inhabitants.

These councils provide all normal local government services. However, such strategic functions as policing, fire services and water supply (water is not privatised in Scotland as it is in the rest of Britain) need to be organised on a larger scale. So a number of **joint boards** have been established. These deal with police (eight areas), water (three), fire (four) and tourism (four).

Although this scheme appears to suggest stability, it must be remembered that devolution of power to a Scottish Assembly will return power over local government affairs to Edinburgh. If dissatisfaction with a structure originally imposed on Scotland from London should emerge, further changes may result.

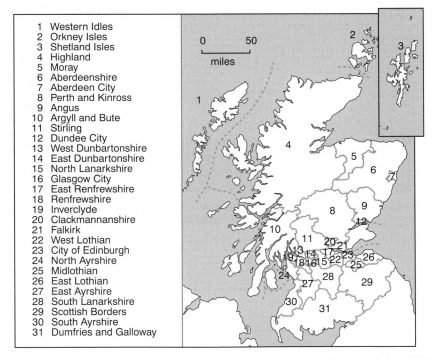

1   Western Idles
2   Orkney Isles
3   Shetland Isles
4   Highland
5   Moray
6   Aberdeenshire
7   Aberdeen City
8   Perth and Kinross
9   Angus
10 Argyll and Bute
11 Stirling
12 Dundee City
13 West Dunbartonshire
14 East Dunbartonshire
15 North Lanarkshire
16 Glasgow City
17 East Renfrewshire
18 Renfrewshire
19 Inverclyde
20 Clackmannanshire
21 Falkirk
22 West Lothian
23 City of Edinburgh
24 North Ayrshire
25 Midlothian
26 East Lothian
27 East Ayrshire
28 South Lanarkshire
29 Scottish Borders
30 South Ayrshire
31 Dumfries and Galloway

NEW LOCAL AUTHORITY AREAS, FOLLOWING THE LOCAL GOVERNMENT ETC (SCOTLAND) ACT 1994

WALES

Here a simpler system was established in 1974. The country was divided into eight first tier counties which were further split into a total of 37 districts. This was, therefore, a simple two tier system. As with Scotland, local communities were given the option of setting up their own councils for very small scale government.

The second phase of change came at the same time as the Scottish reorganisation, 1996. The country was divided into 21 unitary authorities to carry out all local government functions (again the small community councils were retained). As in Scotland, arrangements were set in train for joint boards to handle such services as economic development, policing and the fire services.

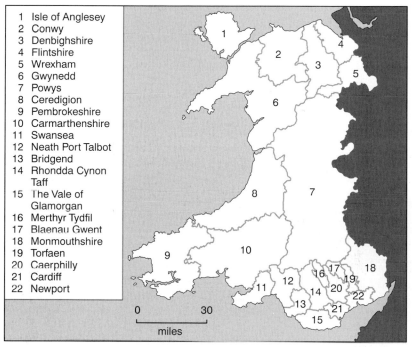

1	Isle of Anglesey
2	Conwy
3	Denbighshire
4	Flintshire
5	Wrexham
6	Gwynedd
7	Powys
8	Ceredigion
9	Pembrokeshire
10	Carmarthenshire
11	Swansea
12	Neath Port Talbot
13	Bridgend
14	Rhondda Cynon Taff
15	The Vale of Glamorgan
16	Merthyr Tydfil
17	Blaenau Gwent
18	Monmouthshire
19	Torfaen
20	Caerphilly
21	Cardiff
22	Newport

NEW UNITARY AUTHORITIES CREATED IN WALES ON 1 APRIL 1997

NORTHERN IRELAND

The structure of sub-central government in Northern Ireland was established in 1972 following the **Macrory Report**. As the modern sectarian disturbances were beginning, it was clear that restructuring was overdue. Three main reasons for change can be identified:

- Northern Ireland has always been governed separately from the rest of Great Britain. Before 1972 it had its own devolved government (known as 'Stormont', described in Chapter 7); after 1972 the province came under the direct rule of

Westminster and the Northern Ireland Office. Thus local government had been responsible for fewer services than local authorities elsewhere. This resulted in small scale operations which were becoming inefficient.

- There was widespread suspicion among the minority Catholic community that local boundaries had been gerrymandered in the past. **Gerrymandering** is the practice of drawing government boundaries in such a way as to favour one political party. Thus a redrawing of boundaries might allay these fears.
- At local level, there were also feelings that small, single-party dominated authorities discriminated against minorities in their communities. This was particularly true of housing and employment practices.

The system was a two tier arrangement, shown in table 4.

Table 4: *Two tier authority in Northern Ireland*		
AUTHORITY	MEMBERSHIP	MAIN FUNCTIONS
9 Area Boards	Partly appointed by the Northern Ireland Office, partly delegates from district councils	Education, planning, health, housing, road transport, family social services
26 District Councils	Directly elected	Environmental services, refuse collection, small scale planning, health inspection, parks and gardens, cemeteries

Not surprisingly, Northern Ireland is treated very differently from the rest of the United Kingdom. Most laws are made by edict of the Northern Ireland Office, as opposed to full parliamentary procedures as take place elsewhere. Its local government is actually regional in nature and largely controlled by officials who are not elected. In fact, elected local politicians there have relatively little power. The deep sectarian conflict and the inability to find consensus on important issues makes this almost inevitable.

Northern Ireland provides us with some sort of model of how regional government might look if it were applied to England. Of course on the mainland it would be both desirable and necessary to place regional government firmly in the hands of elected politicians. The lack of democracy in the province is the result of the breakdown in normal pluralist, liberal politics there.

NORTHERN IRELAND DISTRICT COUNCILS

ENGLAND

The story of local government reorganisation in the national regions may seem convoluted, but when we compare it to the English experience, it appears absurdly simple. As we have seen above, it is a story of discontinuity, indecision, political controversy and general directionless confusion. When Labour came to power in 1997 the picture was still blurred.

Four principal stages can be usefully identified:

- the **Greater London Council**
- the 1974 Reforms
- 1986 – the demise of city regions
- the Local Government Commission, 1992.

The Greater London Council (GLC)

This was set up in 1965 in place of the smaller London County Council (LCC) which had its origins in the nineteenth century. In essence, the GLC was an expansion of the more compact LCC, taking over chunks of the home counties which were formerly Essex, Kent, Middlesex and Surrey. The GLC was divided into 32 boroughs (plus the City of London which had its own peculiar system of self-government).

The principle was that strategic services such as large scale planning, public transport, support for the Arts, emergency services (though not the police who are directly under Home Office control in London), some housing, refuse disposal and a variety of community projects should be controlled by an authority governing the whole capital. The smaller boroughs would control the more personal services such as minor planning, local road maintenance, some housing, social services, libraries, parks and gardens, care of the elderly. Education was also the responsibility of the second tier boroughs, though, as we have already seen, the 12 inner boroughs formed a joint board known as the Inner London Education Authority (ILEA).

THE OLD GLC BUILDING

The GLC experiment came to an acrimonious end in 1986 when it was abolished on the orders of Prime Minister Thatcher. For several years a running battle had raged between a rebellious, leftwing council, led by Ken Livingstone (known as 'Red Ken' at the time) and a government which sought to exert control over local autonomy, especially where financial expenditure was concerned. Despairing of victory, Margaret Thatcher resorted to abolition and she forced it through Parliament against fierce political opposition.

Despite its relatively short life, the GLC provides us with a rare glimpse at the possibilities for regional government. In a sense, although centred on one city, the GLC was a regional body. Its existence was an acceptance that London was the centre of a true region with its own problems of development, transport and culture. It also was a separate economic unit which could and should be treated differently from the rest of the country. It can therefore be considered a paradigm or model of what regional government can achieve, and also what problems it can bring. Table 5 summarises the balance sheet of the GLC, using a number of examples.

Table 5: *GLC achievements and problems*	
ACHIEVEMENTS	PROBLEMS
• Gave London a sense of identity • Some degree of regional transport planning • Encouragement of the Arts at all levels • Strategic planning in low cost housing • Maintenance of a coherent system of public transport	• The creation of a large, expensive bureaucracy • Providing a permanent challenge to the power of central government • Its size could be seen as a hindrance to local democracy, especially lacking accountability • Often in conflict with the London boroughs when they were controlled by a different party

The 1974 reforms

In 1966, the Redcliffe-Maud Committee was set up by the Labour government under Harold Wilson. Its brief was to modernise the structure of local government in England and Wales. It was, indeed part of a broader policy to bring Britain into the modern world which included proposed changes in the civil service, trade unions, higher education and technological development.

The committee reported in 1969, recommending a system of 58 unitary, single tier authorities for most of the country except for three city regions based on Liverpool, Birmingham and Manchester. These would be two tier authorities on the lines of the GLC. Most of these proposals were accepted by the government. However, before action could be taken, Labour lost power in the election of 1970.

The Conservatives produced a compromise plan which accepted the general idea of city regions, but rejected the principle of unitary authorities. It legislated for change in 1972 and the new system came into effect in 1974. The main changes were as follows:

- The GLC concept of 'city regions' was extended to six other areas. Thus, metropolitan counties were set up in Greater Manchester, Merseyside (Liverpool), South Yorkshire (Sheffield), West Yorkshire (Leeds), Tyne and Wear (Newcastle) and West Midlands (Birmingham). These were similar in operation to the GLC.

- Some rationalisation of the other (non-metropolitan) counties took place, eliminating inefficient, 'illogical' counties such as Rutland, the smallest, and creating new large counties such as Avon and Humberside.
- There were 47 two tier authorities. However, the second tier districts had relatively minor functions, certainly less than the London boroughs or the metropolitan boroughs.
- The minor parish system of small scale community democracy was maintained.

The system, which lasted until 1986 is summarised in table 6.

Table 6: *The 1974 reforms*		
FIRST TIER	SECOND TIER	THIRD TIER
Greater London Council (1)	London Boroughs (32)	Parishes (very few)
Metropolitan Counties (6)	Metro. Boroughs (36)	Parishes (very few)
Other Counties (47)	County Districts (333)	Parishes (11,000)

In so far as there was any rationale behind the 1974 reforms, it was to create a system which made economic sense. The units were designed to be the most efficient, given the scale of service which each was to provide. Local sentiment and democratic considerations were of secondary importance.

1986 – the demise of city regions

By the mid 1980s the GLC and the metropolitan counties, all under Labour party control, had tried the patience of Margaret Thatcher to breaking point. She was unable to control their spending levels, believed them to be over-sized, unresponsive bureaucracies and refused to accept their opposition to key policies, especially in education and housing. They were, therefore, abolished.

The functions which they had previously undertaken were mostly transferred down to the second tier authorities. They therefore became single tier local government areas. Some strategic services which needed large scale planning were transferred either to new joint boards (emergency services, refuse disposal), while others were transferred to central government or to voluntary organisations (housing).

Britain's first serious flirtation with the idea of regional government had ended. Abolition was not the result of any long-term vision, however, rather it was a political expediency resulting from local–central tensions.

The Local Government Commission, 1992

At last, it seemed in 1992 that a sense of purpose had entered the world of local government reorganisation. The Secretary of State for the Environment, Michael Heseltine, decided to explore the possibility of moving to a completely single tier system in England. There were clear benefits to be gained from eliminating a whole level of bureaucracy. It would also be easier for people to understand. Heseltine set up the Local Government Commission for England to organise the changes. Its chairman was Sir John Banham.

Matters were progressing reasonably well in 1992–3, when problems in the relationship between the government and the Commission began to emerge. John Gummer took over from Heseltine as the responsible Minister, and decided to put pressure on the Commission to recommend single tiering in all but 'exceptional' cases. This seemed to challenge the independence of the Commission and angered many local government politicians. Two councils – Derbyshire and Lancashire – claimed that Gummer was acting unlawfully in interfering, and instituted legal proceedings. But, even though they won the case in the High Court in January 1994, the Minister made only a cosmetic retraction and continued to press for the unitary solution.

So the early hopes for decisive action were dashed. In the next two months Gummer referred three recommendations for two tier systems in Yorkshire, Lincolnshire and Gloucestershire, back to the Commission. He was still determined to pursue confrontational politics in this field. Matters came to a head in March 1995 when Gummer announced that the Commission should concentrate on the creation of single rather than two tier authorities. The driving force, as usual, was for efficiency rather than local feelings. Sir John Banham promptly resigned in protest. He had insisted that, where local feelings were strong enough, two tier authorities should be retained; the Minister disagreed, so resignation was inevitable. Banham was replaced by Sir David Cooksey.

The Commission may continue to recommend changes in the structure of English local government, but most of its work was complete by 1996 when 46 new unitary and county authorities had been created while the rest of the country (other than the special circumstances of London) was divided into two tier authorities. In the process, four counties were abolished – Avon, Cleveland, Humberside (the three which had come into being in 1974) together with the historical county of Berkshire. Ironically, the much mourned tiny county of Rutland, which had been abolished as an administrative unit in 1974, was restored, accompanied by great local rejoicing.

A note on third tier authorities

These very small authorities, known in England as **parish** or town councils (community councils elsewhere), are the lowest tier of local government which exist in many areas, but rarely in cities.

They have very limited jurisdiction, including such matters as parking regulations in villages, minor planning applications, street lighting and the management of the local environment. They are organised by a clerk, who is not a professional, and are staffed by enthusiastic local residents. Meetings need not be frequent and the responsibility is not onerous. Very often it is difficult to find enough volunteers, especially as political parties seldom become involved with their work. Occasionally town or village meetings may be called on controversial issues to test public opinion. They can, therefore, be a rare example of **direct democracy** operating in Britain.

A new London authority?

In July 1997, the government issued a green (consultative) paper on a future London-wide authority to replace the defunct GLC. This is to be known as the **Greater London Authority** (GLA).

The green paper, largely the inspiration of Deputy Prime Minister John Prescott, leaves no doubt as to the government's attitude towards the issue:

The government believes that for too long, decisions in London have been taken by central government and shadowy committees behind closed doors. Nobody knows who speaks for London and too often nobody does. The new authority will give Londoners a voice which will be listened to at home and abroad. It will be the democratic voice of five million London voters.

'New Leadership for London' *Cm 3724*

In the document's key criteria section, an insight into the Labour government's general attitude to both local and regional government is given. These criteria are listed in table 7.

To some extent, this statement contains political rhetoric, but it also demonstrates a determination to provide London with an effective new authority, which is also limited in size and function. It is a set of criteria which could apply to the Labour government's policy towards all larger scale local government.

This new authority could be a blueprint for new kinds of authorities with a greater degree of independence, but which may also be more democratically accountable. The main features are to be an elected mayor and an elected assembly of 24–32 members. Their respective functions are shown on page 26 in table 8.

This leaves one further question and it is the one which requires the greatest amount of discussion and ultimate agreement: the actual role of the GLA. What local government functions will it undertake? The proposal suggests the following list:

- Land-use planning
- Transport strategy
- Economic development and regeneration
- Environmental protection

- Culture, media and leisure
- Police
- Fire Services
- Other miscellaneous services across London

Should parliament approve the plans for a new GLA, a referendum of Londoners will be held in May 1998. A positive result in such a referendum will result in the authority appearing early in the twenty-first century.

Table 7: *Criteria for the GLA*	
CRITERIA	ROLE
Strategic	Concerned with strategy, thinking and planning for London, particularly at a pan-London and sub-regional level.
Democratic	Directly elected by the people of London, and accountable, with clear and public objectives and targets, reporting regularly to the electorate on progress.
Inclusive	Involving relevant interests such as business, boroughs, the voluntary sector and ethnic minorities in planning and implementation.
Effective	Promoting, leading and empowered to take practical action to bring about change
Small	Streamlined in terms of staff, the numbers of assembly members and cost.
Audible	With a high profile role for the mayor, speaking up for London and promoting London's interests particularly in the international context.
Consensual	Building a consensus, taking a pragmatic approach, working with the grain, confident within its area of responsibility.
Clear about its role	Avoiding duplication of responsibilities and simplifying existing structures and government.
Efficient	Using its resources to best effect, reflecting the government's commitment to achieve best value.
Influential	Capable of influencing policy formulation and decision-making in a range of public and private sector organisations.

SOURCE: DEPARTMENT OF THE ENVIRONMENT CM 3724, JULY 1997

Table 8: *The proposed elected bodies for London*	
MAYOR	ASSEMBLY
• Devising and proposing the annual budget	• Approving the annual budget
• Developing and promoting strategic plans for London	• Approving appointments proposed by the mayor
• Being a spokesperson for London, both in Britain and abroad	• Making the mayor accountable
• Proposing permanent appointments in the authority	• Making permanent officers and London organisation accountable with the power to summon witnesses from London bodies in their investigations

SUMMARY

Although the history of local government structure appears to be haphazard and confusing, there are a number of principles and patterns which can be stressed:

- The three factors which have been considered are: what is the most efficient size of authority which is appropriate to each function of local government? how can the requirements of democracy be best served? what kind of administrative units do communities wish to see preserved?
- Despite these three considerations, there has been a general drift towards the principle of unitary, single tier authorities in the United Kingdom.
- The process represents a good illustration of how lack of consensus and continuity in modern British politics can hold back progress towards the creation of better government.
- Despite protestations of objectivity, party politicians cannot resist the temptation to interfere with local government organisation in the interests of their party's broader aims.

STUDY GUIDE

Notes should be organised on the following key areas:

- What are the factors which are taken into consideration in creating a structure? These will centre on history, efficiency and democratic considerations.
- The key facts in the history of the structure should be identified. In each case the changes should be measured against the three criteria shown above (p 12).
- Why have there been so many changes in the structure? The important factors have been lack of political continuity, lack of consensus on aims and a general tendency for central government to view local government as an inferior level of governance. In this regard there should be some synthesis with the material on local–central relations which are covered later.
- Construct a set of arguments in favour of, and against the restoration of big city strategic authorities, both in London and elsewhere. This may be extended to a scheme of assessment of the value of elected city mayors.

Exam hints

Most questions centre on the issue of size and the relative merits of large or small authorities. Good answers will contain the following features:

- What are the key criteria in assessing size?
- What lessons can be learned from recent political developments in the field?
- How will the development of regional government affect the issue?
- What significance might the growing importance of the EU bring?
- A strong conclusion should offer firm suggestions as to which criteria are most important in determining a rational, democratic structure.

Practice Questions

1 a Why were the Greater London Council, the Inner London Education Authority and six other metropolitan counties abolished in the 1980s?
  b What arguments can be advanced for the restoration of metropolitan authorities, especially in London?
2 a What changes have been made in the structure of local governments in the 1990s?
  b Why have these changes been made?
3 Evaluate the relative merits of arguments which suggest that local authorities should be **a** as small as possible, or **b** as large as possible.

3

HOW LOCAL AUTHORITIES WORK

Introduction

THIS CHAPTER WILL build up a picture of how the normal local authority operates. There are small variations from one authority to another, especially at different levels of government. However most aspects of organisation are common to all authorities.

A number of questions need to be addressed:

- How are authorities organised to make decisions?
- How do the various personalities relate to one another?
- What are their powers and responsibilities?

In addition, a number of issues which arise from organisation and internal power relationships will be considered.

As we have already seen, the nature of local government in Britain is undergoing constant change. Its relationships with national and international bodies are being transformed; devolved regional government is being developed and other new decision-making organisations, mostly quangos, are constantly being created. There are, therefore, also questions of how internal arrangements may have to alter to meet these new challenges.

Key Points

This chapter contains material on the following key issues:

- The internal structure of local authorities, including how decisions are made and where power lies.
- The relationship between elected councillors and the permanent, professional officers of the council.

- The nature of party control.
- The variety of issues surrounding the work of councillors.

DEFINITIONS

The principal individuals and bodies are now defined:

THE LOCAL AUTHORITY

A general term, referring to the whole organisation which has been authorised (hence the name 'authority') to:

- make certain defined decisions
- allocate resources
- enforce regulations or by-laws
- organise the provision of services within a defined territory.

Authorisation is granted either by Parliament through legislation, or by central government ministers under powers granted to them by Parliament. The term 'authority' includes both elected councillors and permanent, non-elected officials.

The term is also sometimes split in order to define a specific function – we may speak of the 'local education authority' or the 'planning authority'. These expressions refer to those councillors and officers who have been authorised to administer those particular services.

THE COUNCIL

This is very specifically the elected part of the authority. There is a variable number of elected councillors. Most (but not all) councillors are members of a political party. When the whole council meets we may refer to 'plenary' session.

THE COMMITTEES

These are made up of a smaller number of elected councillors, although they may also co-opt non-councillors representing other groups in the area. These co-opted members may take part in discussions and sometimes have voting rights (though not in full council). Each key function of the authority will have a committee dealing with its operation. There are also sub-committees for more detailed work.

LOCAL GOVERNMENT OFFICERS

These are not elected but are appointed on a permanent basis. They are expected to be politically neutral. Councillors are part-time amateurs so there must be full time professionals to run an authority. The most senior officer is Chief Executive of the authority (they used to be known as Town Clerks). Each section of the authority will be headed by a Chief Officer, usually known as Director. The senior officers are appointed by the councillors, but lower officials are appointed through a normal process of professional recruitment.

PARTY GROUPS

Those councillors who represent a political party (nearly all in large authorities, less in the smaller areas) meet regularly to determine the local party's view on each issue. They will try to reach (but cannot enforce) a common position on each issue before decisions are made. Each party group elects a leader. Where one party enjoys a majority in the council its leader is normally known as 'Leader of the Council'.

THE MAYOR

Up to 1998, the position of mayor has been a purely honorary, ceremonial position. There are proposals for change, but up to that year it was a post held by a long serving councillor of the majority party, who is given the honour as a mark of respect for many years of unpaid service to the community.

We can now consider these elements in more detail, describe their functions and discuss how they relate to each other.

INTERNAL STRUCTURE

The most convenient way to view the way in which local authorities work is to characterise it as three pillars. These are shown in table 9 with a brief description of their role. We can now examine each of these pillars in turn:

PARTY GROUPS

In the last three decades of the twentieth century, there has been a steady increase in the influence which local party organisations have sought to exert over local government. There used to be a romanticised image of the independent councillor, who might have received help from his party in getting elected, but who then considered himself a free agent, doing what s/he thought best for his or her community. Why is this so? There are a number of reasons:

- The steady increase in the responsibilities of local government since the Second World War has meant that more political gains, in terms of the achievements of party objectives, are on offer in the local sphere.

Table 9: *The three pillars of local authority*		
PARTY GROUPS	COUNCILLORS	OFFICERS
Determining local party policy within the confines of the powers and responsibilities of the authority.	Making decisions and giving guidance either in full council or in committees.	Giving policy advice, carrying out research, recommending action, organising the implementation of decisions made by councillors and overseeing the work of agencies contracted to undertake the authority's responsibilities.

- Since about 1970, there has been an intensification in adversary politics. To some extent this has spilled over into local affairs.
- Opposition parties have regarded local politics as an opportunity to defy the will of central government at times when Ministers have been able to control Parliament completely.
- Local government is an increasingly complex operation. The enthusiastic, independent-minded amateur councillor may find some issues technically difficult to deal with. There is, therefore, inevitably greater reliance on the support which parties can give.
- A number of local government issues which were formerly the subject of cross-party agreements (consensus politics) had become matters of great political controversy. Among them were education, housing and policing.

This trend was confirmed by the report of the **Widdicome Committee** in 1986. The Committee was alarmed by a series of events in which there was an apparently excessive amount of party control exercised over local government, and a danger of central government becoming thwarted by local political action. A selection of examples may illustrate the problem:

Council rents

In 1972 the Labour-led council in Clay Cross in Derbyshire refused to implement the Housing Finance Act. This required them to raise the level of council house rents in order to relieve the financial burden on taxpayers. The councillors were overruled and fined for their actions.

Comprehensive education

In the late 1970s, the Labour government was seeking to introduce non-selective, comprehensive secondary education in all areas. They attempted to do this without legislation at first. A number of Conservative-controlled authorities defied this policy, despite the fact that there was widespread support for the measure. By resorting to legal action to assert their independence, these authorities were able to delay implementation until Labour had lost power.

Housing

The Housing Act 1980 required local authorities to offer council-controlled dwellings for sale to their tenants at discount prices. Labour-controlled Norwich Council deliberately obstructed the programme on the grounds that they were politically opposed to it. Only severe threats to the councillors in 1982 persuaded them to comply.

The GLC

Led by Labour leftwinger Ken Livingstone, the GLC waged a campaign in the early 1980s to maintain high levels of expenditure in the social interests of London, against the clear policy of the government of reining in public spending. This ultimately led, as we have seen, to the abolition of the GLC in 1986.

Several other Labour-led councils, such as Islington, Lambeth and Liverpool also pursued their own political agenda against the authority of central government. Furthermore, many were controlled by a clandestine group of Marxist-inspired activists known as **Militant Tendency**. In many cases, the individuals who were running local policy were not even elected councillors.

The Widdicombe Committee recommended a number of reforms to try to loosen party control of authorities, but most were too weak for Prime Minister Thatcher. She preferred more draconian methods to bring defiant councils to heel:

- The abolition of the GLC and the metropolitan counties. They were all Labour-controlled and were the most difficult to control.
- By tightening legislative and ministerial control, so that opportunities for party groups to pursue their own policies were steadily reduced.
- Controls over spending and borrowing were made more stringent.
- The process was instituted of removing control over key services from councils altogether. In some cases these were transferred to government-appointed quangos or to private and voluntary organisations which were not party-dominated.

Supplementing these active measures, three other developments were taking place which also reduced party political influence over local authorities:

- Under the leadership of Neil Kinnock, the Labour Party in the later 1980s was able to curb or remove entirely the leftwing elements in the party.
- The growing electoral successes of the Liberal Democrats in the 1980s and 90s meant that progressively fewer councils were coming under the absolute majority control of either of the main parties. Forced to share power with the third party, councillors were obliged to maintain more moderate policies and to accept compromise positions.

- A key recommendation of the Widdicombe report – that local government officers should never be appointed on political grounds – began to affect the degree to which party groups could exert control over policy.

By the end of the 1990s, we can see a local government system which is far less party-influenced than it had been over the previous 30 years. Table 10 indicates how, in recent local elections, a reasonable number of councils were not under single party control; ie, where there was no overall majority for any party, or independent councillors were in a majority. Though the number of councils under party control is relatively large, there is still a substantial minority where there is no overall party control, especially in rural England.

Table 10: *Party control of councils in recent elections*			
REGION AND DATE	NO. OF COUNCILS CONTROLLED BY THE PARTY	REGION AND DATE	NO. OF COUNCILS CONTROLLED BY THE PARTY
London 1994		**England 1997***	
Labour	17	Labour	19
Conservative	4	Lib. Dem.	3
Lib. Dem.	3	Conservative	10
No overall control	8	No overall control	18
Wales 1995		**Scotland 1994**	
Labour	14	Labour	4
Independent	4	Independent	5
Plaid Cymru**	1	No overall control	3
No overall control	3		

*NON-METROPOLITAN (RURAL) COUNTIES AND UNITARY AUTHORITIES ONLY
**THE WELSH NATIONALIST PARTY

Parties *do* still seek to run local authorities, but they are no longer in a position to dominate as they once did.

COUNCILLORS

Since 1989, local authorities have had the opportunity to pay leading councillors, such as council leaders and committee chairpersons, fairly substantial annual retainers (the sums are not large enough to be described as a salary). These are in addition to allowances made for each daily attendance at the council or one of its committees. While this has enabled or encouraged more people to become councillors, the financial rewards remain too small for the introduction of full time professionals.

Councillors are therefore essentially part-time amateurs. They give up large amounts of time – estimates vary between about 50–100 hours per month – from a sense of duty, to achieve social status or to pursue political aims. Though most meetings take place in the evenings, there are still a number of sessions during normal working hours. Some groups are therefore effectively disqualified from working in local government. Those who are retired, who rely on others for their source of income or are self-employed, may have time on their hands. Others, however, must rely on the goodwill of employers to be able to attend enough meetings to justify membership.

Should full-time professional councillors be introduced? This has been considered from time to time, and the Widdicombe report certainly suggested larger payments. However, there has been no serious attempt to professionalise councils. The arguments for and against full-timers are summarised in table 11.

Table 11: *Full-time councillors?*	
For	Against
• It would enable a wider variety of people to become involved • Councillors would have the time to become more informed in the business of government • There may be a reduced chance that they will become financially corrupt in order to compensate them for their time • They would have more time to deal with the interests of their constituents	• Authorities already have professional officers. Paid councillors might duplicate their work • It would be extremely expensive as there are many thousands of councillors • It is better to have councillors who spend more of their time living and working in the community as they will understand local problems better. Professionals might become remote from the community • It might attract people who are not genuinely committed to public service

What do councillors do? The answer is surprisingly varied. The list shown below indicates the large number of roles which councillors *may* undertake. Of course some are more committed and therefore busier than others, but all of the following activities are normal:

- Attending party group meetings to determine policy. This is especially important if they are members of a majority, ruling party which is likely to be able to force its policies through the council.
- Attending full plenary sessions of the council, occasionally contributing to debates.
- Attending council committee and sub-committee meetings. This is the principal aspect of the councillor's role. Much of the important business is done in these specialised committees.
- Reading information and preparing for full council and committee meetings.
- Dealing with individual problems raised by their constituents, typically problems with housing, planning applications or education.
- Representing the council and their party on external bodies which require local authority participation. Examples include school boards of governors and health authorities.
- Occasionally representing the interests of the council at central government level or through a local MP.
- Some may be members of local pressure groups such as conservationists, residents' associations, chambers of commerce or neighbourhood watches.
- Attending public occasions and functions on a ceremonial basis.

A LOCAL COUNCIL IN SESSION

This is an exhausting list, and no doubt practising councillors could add a few more examples of their duties! When we consider that most councillors undertake these functions while also earning their own living, we can appreciate how arduous their role can be. Table 12 gives some idea of what kinds of people typically become councillors.

Table 12: *Occupations of councillors*	
OCCUPATIONAL GROUP	PERCENTAGE OF TOTAL
Professional	9
Employers/senior managers	32
Intermediate managers	18
Junior managers and office workers	10
Skilled manual	16
Semi-skilled manual	4
Unskilled manual	1
Former armed forces	11

SOURCE: WIDDICOMBE REPORT 1986

As mentioned above, the elected councillors are often supplemented by co-opted members who have not been elected. They are either individuals who are considered to have something to offer but cannot be full-time councillors; others are representatives of local groups such as parents' associations (for education), teacher union delegates, local businessmen, and professionals. Normally they do not take part in full council meetings; their work is largely in specialised committees where knowledge and expertise are needed.

OFFICERS

As we have seen above, local government officers are full-time professionals whose careers lie in local government service. At the top level positions include the Chief Executive, directors of Education, Planning and Social Services. Lower down, there is an army of clerical officers and other minor operatives.

Though they may be members of a political party, they are expected to be politically neutral and, like central government civil servants, must serve the council faithfully, whoever may be in control. However, their relationship with party politicians is not as simple as it may seem. They must be aware of both the policies of the council and the limitations, set by Parliament and government ministers, within which all authorities must operate. Indeed, it is part of their role to explain to councillors just what they can and cannot do.

While the junior officers need not concern us too much since they work largely under procedures set for them by their superiors, we do need to examine the work of the principal officers. They are required to undertake the following tasks, aided by members of their department:

- Advising the elected councillors. This will include information about what requirements are being placed upon the local authority by central government, suggesting what local measures need to be taken and ways of going about it.
- Liaising with central government departments or other administrative bodies which may impinge upon his or her section's work.
- Identifying problems which need to be dealt with and suggesting options for solutions to those problems.
- Ensuring that the committees and sub-committees (especially their chairpersons) which deal with their area of responsibility are properly organised and are provided with necessary information.
- Organising the implementation of the council's decisions.
- Granting contracts to private and voluntary organisations which may be operating services on behalf of the council. Thereafter monitoring the performance of such organisations.
- Managing the department's financial budget in the interests of efficiency and quality of service.

An example of how a department works can be illustrated in the form of a web of relationships shown below. In this case, the operations of the Director of Education are used.

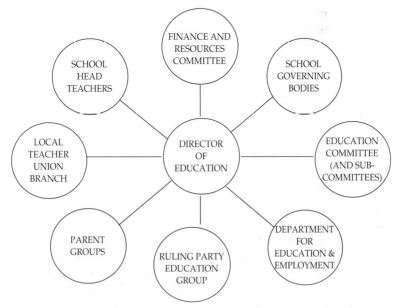

THE DIRECTOR OF EDUCATION – A POLITICAL WEB

Until about 25 years ago, the debate concerning the role of the senior officers centred upon the question of whether they exerted too much political influence over the councillors. Their superior expertise, knowledge and professional status gave them huge advantages over amateur, part-time elected representatives. This was followed by a period of concern, which is described above, when local party groups had gained excessive control over local government. Far from being in a position to control local authorities, the officers complained that they were subject to unacceptable political interference.

Four modern developments have affected their role in particular:

- Today, local authorities are expected to operate increasingly as if they were commercial organisations.
- A wide variety of services are now being provided by private and voluntary organisations over which the council has only partial control.
- Central government direction of local authorities' work is tighter than it has ever been.
- The general culture of government has changed so that citizens are being treated by administrators as customers or clients rather than merely subjects.

All this means that local government officers act today as business managers rather than bureaucrats. They deal largely with issues which have commercial rather than political solutions. Thus, on the one hand they have restored their advantages over councillors, but on the other, their field of discretion has been considerably narrowed.

WHERE DOES THE POWER LIE?

It may seem inevitable that the plenary sessions of local councils are the key to an understanding of how authorities work. However, just as it is an error to believe that central government's business revolves around Parliament, so we must look beyond plenary sessions for our understanding of where the power is located. The problem is that local authorities have no equivalent of the 'Cabinet' and there are no executive ministers as such. It is difficult, therefore to find any central locus of power.

There are a number of candidates:

1 The Council Leader, for example, together with his party group, but this is only true when a single party controls council. Furthermore such groups cannot rely upon the support of all the party's representatives on council as Westminster's whips invariably can.
2 The Chief Executive is in a central position; perhaps s/he is the key figure. In administrative terms this may be true, but s/he still remains the servant of his or her political masters.

3 There is a central committee, known as the Policy and Resources Committee. This, as its title suggests, has the role of considering the financial affairs of the authority and proposes the way in which resources should be allocated among the different functions. It seems, therefore, that we are nearing the end of our search. Certainly this committee, and its chairperson in particular, forms a powerful alliance with the Chief Executive and the Director of Finance, but it still does not exercise complete political control.

The answer is, in fact, that there is no centre of power. Rather, there are a number of key locations. It is probably most accurate to think of the council committees in general, together with the individuals and bodies which surround them. You can think of an authority as a series of 'power triangles', with committees as their pivot.

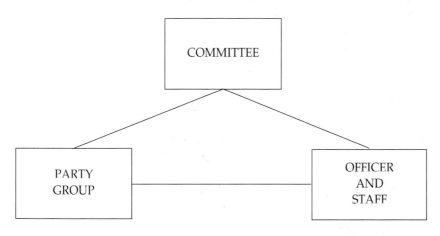

CouncilCommittees – power triangles

Councils are not like Parliament. They meet relatively infrequently and for short periods. Thus, they cannot possibly deal with all the business of the authority in any realistic detail. They must reserve their time for the more controversial and strategic decisions or simply to approve recommendations emerging from the committees. It is, then, in the committees and their sub-divisions that the details of council business are covered. The key issues are resolved there and if they cannot be, matters are referred back to the officers for more consideration. By the time the full council meets, there is rarely anything left to discuss.

The political make-up of the whole council is reflected in each committee so ruling parties or **coalitions** of parties are able to exercise political influence over the committees too. Committees are politically directed by these party groups, administratively guided by the relevant officers and lobbied by external pressure groups who have a vested interest in their decisions. So we have now discovered where much of the power is located.

ELECTED MAYORS?

There are a number of reforms in local government in prospect following the election of a Labour government in 1997. Here we will concentrate on one possibility, potentially the most far-reaching in its effects.

Inspiration for this idea stems largely from the experience of the United States of America and of France. In those political systems the big city mayors are dominant political figures, both for positive reasons (in the past, Chirac in Paris and Cuomo in New York) and for negative reasons as with the notoriously allegedly corrupt Tapie in Marseilles and Daley in Chicago. In addition, the loss of the GLC in 1986 led to fears that the capital was losing a sense of identity. A mayor of London (the Lord Mayor of London is merely an honorary representative of the financial City of London) was suggested as a sort of replacement for a London-wide authority.

Powerful, accountable mayors have been able to achieve a number of effects in other political systems, some of which might be reproduced in Britain. These include:

- giving the community a sense of identity and focus
- counterbalancing the authority of non-elected officials
- representing the interests of the city to central government ministers
- encouraging a positive electoral mandate for change through an individual who is also accountable directly to the electorate
- creating a strategic vision of how a city should operate; eg, in fields such as transport, planning, economic development, cultural activity, environmental improvement and education
- the possibility that an individual may be able to represent the city on a non-partisan basis (even if the mayor him/herself may be a party member)
- presenting a positive image of the city of the rest of the country and abroad, including in the EU.

The government's Green Paper on a new authority for London (Dept of the Environment Cm 3724) suggests a new position very much along these lines. In addition it is stated Labour Party policy that other large communities should also have the opportunity to elect a mayor. It is proposed that local referenda (including in London) should determine whether the community desires such a development.

SUMMARY

We can now identify three periods of development in the nature of local authority organisation in modern times:

BUREAUCRATIC MANAGEMENT AND THE BAINS REPORT

Encouraged by the findings of the Bains Report in 1972 which extolled the virtues of efficient, civil service style management by local government officers, the 1970s was a period in which elected councillors were very much dominated by their professional masters. Indeed, so great was this domination that fears were expressed that local democracy was being subverted by professional managers who cared less for accountability and more for administrative convenience. Underpaid and underinformed councillors could not hope to rival the power of the permanent bureaucracies.

In the big cities in particular, powerful Chief Executives or 'City Managers' as they were often known, were able to dominate local politics to the detriment of the much weaker elected representatives. In Newcastle, T. Dan Smith was the most notable example of the all-powerful manager who exercised control on an American scale through **patronage** and control of huge budgets (Smith was ultimately ousted for corruption but left his mark on the city and this new style of city politics).

POLITICS TAKES OVER IN THE 1980s

From the late 1970s into the 1980s, there emerged a new breed of councillor at a time when central government began to exert tighter controls over local administration. This councillor saw local politics as a means by which an increasingly rightwing, **neo-liberal** government could be defied. The weakness of the Labour opposition in this period was ironically juxtaposed against the growing strength of the party at local level. Voters who were prepared to support the Conservative Party at Westminster balanced the picture by continually electing Labour councils, at least in the towns and cities of England, Wales and Scotland.

To the growing alarm of ministers, party groups wrested control of many authorities from the officers, and implemented programmes directly opposed to Cabinet policies. The Widdicombe Report of 1986 confirmed these fears. Although Widdicombe was anxious that politicians continued to make key decisions, the committee was concerned that local party groups were seeking to control local politics in their own interest, rather than those of the community.

Though the Widdicombe Report itself made relatively little practical impact, it coincided with a period, in the second half of the 1980s, when party influence was beginning to decline.

EQUILIBRIUM IN THE 1990s

As the powers and independence of local government waned in the 1990s, and the Labour Party purged its own militant leftwing, a new balance appeared in the relationship between elected councillors and professional managers. Indeed, an **Audit Commission** report in 1990 pointed the way to a clearer demarcation of roles.

As the work of local government changed, from being managers of services rather than direct providers (a process described fully in Chapter 5) it was clear that councillors could not be intimately concerned with the day-to-day running of an increasingly technical operation. Inevitably, then, they were required only to make strategic decisions which would give the council's work its general direction. Management itself had to be left to the officers who were themselves becoming less bureaucratic and more commercial.

For the moment there is a calm balance as the Audit Commission had hoped. How much Labour reforms, especially the introduction of elected mayors, may disturb this equilibrium in the next century, remains to be seen.

STUDY ⊕ GUIDE

Revision hints

There is a considerable variety of issues here. A clear picture of the following questions should be reduced to a condensed form:

- What is the committee system and why is it so important? Include such features as the complexity of business, the part-time character of councillors and the relationship between councillors and officers.
- What is the nature of the relationship between councillors and officers? List the features of the roles of each. Consider the requirements of democracy and of efficiency which may conflict with each other.
- Construct a balance sheet of how important a part 'politics' should play in local government. On the positive side, refer to such factors as democracy, accountability and clear direction. Against this, list the dangers of interference by local party groups and the possibility that political controversy might jeopardise efficient provision of services.
- A similar pros and cons set of notes should be produced on the question of whether councillors should become full-time professionals.

The key question concerns the influence of politics, and whether services such as education, social services and planning should be subject to party politics. Strong answers will consider the requirements of democratic local government against the drive for efficiency and quality of service. Consideration should also be given to the increasing control which central government has exercised in the field. You should ask whether there is any room left for local politics. Illustrations should be used from the recent history of local government, such as the GLC story and the local–central battles of the 1980s.

The question of professional councillors can be largely covered in a discussion of the role of local authorities. If there is to be genuine local autonomy with councillors playing a key role in decision-making, there may be a good case for professionals. If, on the other hand, they are merely a democratic element in what is an increasingly commercial-style operation, their amateur, part-time status may be appropriate. A similar approach can be adopted in questions about the relationships between councillors and officers.

1 a What is the 'committee system' in local government?
   b Should it be replaced by a cabinet system along the lines of central government?
2 Are decisions in local government best made by elected councillors or by professional officers?
3 What arguments can be advanced for the introduction of professional, full-time local councillors?

4

LOCAL GOVERNMENT FINANCE

Introduction

'HE WHO PAYS the piper calls the tune', may be a cliché, but, like most clichés, it is often true. This is especially so in the field of local government. Finance is crucial throughout government, of course, but at local level the way in which services are paid for is particularly influential. There are a considerable number of ways in which local authorities raise money, each of which carries its own problems and opportunities. In short, you cannot hope to understand it fully unless you can get to grips with the intricacies of finance.

Two basic questions should be answered if we are to reach such an understanding:

1 How much flexibility do local authorities have in determining how much revenue they can raise and the manner in which they raise it?
2 How free are they to decide how that revenue may be spent?

There is a correlation between the answer to these two questions; not a complete one, but a very strong link nonetheless. In general, where an authority has the freedom to raise its own funds, it also has a good deal of discretion as to how it is spent. Conversely, where revenue is coming from elsewhere – usually central government – its hands will be largely tied by restrictions and special requirements.

We should not, therefore, see finance as a marginal issue either in local or regional government. On the contrary, it is a central theme and must be treated as such.

Key points

This chapter contains material on the following key issues:

- The various sources of local government revenue, in particular local taxation and the Poll Tax.
- The organisation of expenditure, what are its main elements, and what controls are exercised over this spending.
- The recent history of the tightening of central government control over local finances.
- How the financial position of local government may change under the Labour government elected in 1997.

REVENUE

There are many sources of revenue, including:

- local taxation
- central government grants
- fees and charges
- borrowing.

LOCAL TAXATION

Council Tax

The main form of local revenue-raising is known as **Council Tax**. Britain is unusual in two regards:

1 It has only one means of raising funds locally, ie on property, either dwelling or commercial. In many countries there is more than one source of such revenue; in the USA, for example, there is a variety of taxes in the different state systems, including sales, property and income taxes as the most common.
2 The great reliance on property taxation is uncommon. The most popular system in Europe is local income tax, followed by sales taxes.

It is perhaps understandable that property tax is the method used, in view of the traditionally high value placed in Britain upon ownership of private dwellings. On the European continent, renting property is more popular and there is certainly a weaker reliance upon the private housing market. Apart from a brief flirtation with a form of *per capita* tax between 1988–92, the notorious and ill-fated **Poll Tax** or **Community Charge** to give it its correct name, Britain has always taxed property for local funding.

The traditional system of rates existed for centuries and formed the basis whereby the wealthier classes contributed to local administration, especially poor law relief (welfare). Council Tax is similar to the rates, so there has been relatively little change in this area for many years.

Council Tax is calculated and raised as follows:

- Each home is placed on a 'band' from A to H, depending on its market value.
- Agents operating on behalf of government assess these values, though householders may appeal against their banding.
- The higher the home is banded, the more annual tax is paid.
- Each local taxing authority sets the tax per home, depending on its valuation. If only one person lives in the home there is a rebate of 25 per cent, but two or more occupants are charged the same amount.

Various low income groups may, of course, apply to the Benefits Agency for financial help with the tax, while students and the disabled also receive rebates. As an indication of its level, the average charge for a Band D (middle range) house in year 1997–8 in England and Wales was £678 per annum.

In this way, there is some account taken of the financial circumstances of the taxpayers, in so far as the value of your home reflects your financial means. Nevertheless, it is not *strictly* based on income and has been criticised for that reason. It also depends upon an arbitrary valuation of one's property which may vary according to local conditions, while the inhabitants' income remains constant.

You may also have noticed that there is a potential anomaly here. In prosperous areas such as the Surrey commuter belt or the Cheshire outskirts of Manchester, there is a great deal of valuable housing. In these districts, therefore, the Council Tax revenue will be very high. Furthermore, in such affluent communities there is a lower need for government expenditure, with less social problems and fewer children relying on state education. Thus the local taxation system might exaggerate variations in economic advantages. In response, central government makes an adjustment calculation so that its own grants (see below) will compensate for shortfalls in tax revenue and higher demands on local expenditure in such poorer areas as low-cost housing estates in Liverpool or Glasgow.

Taxation on private dwellings has long been a matter of controversy in British political life. The short and violent history of the Poll Tax is recounted below, but the long-term debate has centred upon the possibility of the introduction of local income tax. For the time being there is agreement between the Conservative and Labour parties that Council Tax works well. Liberal Democrats favour income tax as the fairest system, and they are supported by many others. There are, however, several practical problems in levying such a tax. It is more difficult to assess and collect than property tax – people move around whereas property does not. This simple truth militates against the introduction of local income tax and makes property levies more attractive.

The less obvious issue concerns accountability. Central government taxation acts very much as a political discipline upon Westminster. Citizens are very sensitive to how much central government tax, mostly income tax and VAT, they pay and are willing to punish governments which they think are taxing and spending extravagantly. They do this by simply voting them out of office as Labour found in 1979. This has not been the case at local level. Much to the frustration of central government ministers, there has been relatively little relationship between the voting habits of the electorate and the level of local tax and spending. In other words, the tax system does not make local councillors accountable for their financial conduct. This problem is discussed further below in the section on local democracy.

The Uniform Business Rate (UBR)

This is also known as the National Non-Domestic Rate (NNDR), and is taxation on commercial properties such as shops, offices, factories and workshops. As with housing, the tax depends upon the value of the property in terms of its capacity for business earnings. There, however, the similarity ends. Since 1989 in Scotland and 1990 in the rest of Britain, the rate has been set for the *whole country* by central government.

Because local councils no longer have the power to vary the level of this form of tax, it can really be considered as part of central government's contribution to local revenue. It is *collected* by the local authority, but they cannot use it with any flexibility. Once again the central government grant is adjusted to compensate for those communities which have few commercial premises which can contribute to revenue.

Thus, although Council Tax and UBR appear to be similar, they must be treated very differently from the point of view of analysis. The former is a potential source of local government discretion, the latter is not. However, the Labour government is committed to reviewing commercial rates, and there may be a return to local variation in the future as part of a general policy to give councils more power and freedom of action.

Precepts

We must now address the question of what happens when there are two tiers of local government in a region. It could be that each tier would collect the taxes it needed to top up its other sources of revenue. But this would be inefficient, potentially expensive and confusing. It is therefore agreed that only one tier should collect Council Tax and the revenue should then be divided between the tiers (sometimes three when parish or community councils are present).

Thus, tax is collected by one tier – county councils in England, boroughs in London, district councils in Northern Ireland – following which a grant or **precept** is handed over to the other tiers to cover the services they must provide.

An assessment of local taxation

Before turning to other forms of revenue, it is important to review the main issues concerning local taxation. It will continue to be a source of controversy, especially with the introduction of regionally devolved government (Scotland will be able to establish its own forms of local taxation) and the Labour government review of local government democracy.

In considering any form of taxation we should address the following issues:

- How fair is the tax? Is it based strictly or only loosely on a person's ability to pay?
- Is it easy to collect? Will the costs of collection outweigh any other advantages it may have?
- Is it easy to evade? Again, the losses from evasion may outweigh other factors.
- Will it help to make councillors financially accountable to their electorates?
- How much discretion does it give to councillors to vary the level of revenue they receive?
- Does it cause any discrimination against areas where incomes are lower?

No form of tax can satisfy all these requirements satisfactorily, but it remains the role of policy-makers to achieve as many of these objectives as possible.

CENTRAL GOVERNMENT GRANTS

There are three types of grant:

1 Specific grants
2 A block grant known as the Revenue Support Grant
3 Challenge Funding

All are set by central government ministers, though the total sum available each year for local authorities is determined in the Chancellor of the Exchequer's annual Budget in November (or early December).

The size of central grants has tended to rise during the twentieth century despite occasional blips. This is the result of two trends:

- There has been a steady increase in local government expenditure. It was felt that this was placing an unacceptably heavy burden on local property owners (remember that local taxation has nearly always been paid by property owners and businesses alone). By increasing central grants rather than local taxes, therefore, the load has been transferred from such property owners to taxpayers *in general*.
- There has been a growing desire by ministers to control what local government does. By developing an increasing reliance upon financial support from central government, they have been able to exert increasing domination.

Specific grants

As their name suggests, these are given for the financing of particular services based on an assessment of needs. Among the purposes of specific grants are policing, emergency services, student grants (before their replacement by loans) and most schools' expenditure.

The reason why local and joint authorities are given no discretion in these areas is that the services are considered to be so vital, and must be supplied on a uniform basis throughout the country, that a set standard must be maintained. Needless to say, the effect is to remove local flexibility. The room for manoeuvre by local councillors is almost totally absent. They therefore become mere agents for central government administration, adding a democratic element, but are hardly local decision-makers in those services covered by specific grants.

The Revenue Support Grant

Since 1980 the principle has been established that local authorities should be given a large 'block grant' and that local councils would have free choice as to how it should be used among different services.

When it was introduced by Michael Heseltine, it was heralded as a major advance in local self-government. However, all was not as it seemed. Three factors inhibited the descretionary powers which the extensive transfer from specific to general grants apparently introduced:

- Although a number of services are not covered by specific grants, those which appear to be discretionary are, in fact, so circumscribed by legislation and by ministerial controls that there is little flexibility.
- The Standard Spending Assessment (see below for more detail) sets a minimum quality of service below which an authority must not fall. It also sets an effective top limit on expenditure on each service. This is because if a council spends more of its Revenue Support Grant on one service than the assessment stipulates, it is likely that they will have to reduce expenditure elsewhere. The effect of such switching is likely to be that one or more services will fall below the acceptable standard. It is in practice a straitjacket rather than a freeing-up of controls as was originally suggested.
- If ministers believe that irresponsible overspending has occurred in a particular area, they have the option of introducing penalties. In such an event, the following year's grant could be reduced.

Challenge Funding

This is a relatively modern development and as yet represents a minor element in the field of grants. To what extent the Labour government will use such funding, remains to be seen. Essentially, an annual sum of money is made available and authorities (or groups of authorities for regional plans) may compete for capital grants. They make a proposal for a scheme to the Department of the Environment who will then allocate funds to the most worthy submissions. Education and transport development projects are typical.

For three years from 1997–8 onwards, £600 million is available for such Challenge Funding.

The importance of central grants

The balance of revenue between grants and local taxation reflects to some extent the balance of power between central government and local councils; the ability of local authorities to raise their own taxation gives them some control over their own activities. Grants, on the other hand, represent central control and loss of local discretion.

In general we can identify three key principles:

1 Where a grant is specific it is being used to ensure that there is a degree of *uniformity* of service in different parts of the country.
2 Block (Revenue Support) grants allow some local choice and flexibility, but are so tightly based upon the Standard Spending Assessment of need that there is relatively little room for manoeuvre.
3 Services which are expected to be financed from sources of revenue which are alternatives to grants, especially taxation, remain the main opportunity for local choice and variation.

OTHER REVENUE SOURCES

Fees and charges

Although most local authority services are provided 'free' (charged for out of revenue), there are a number of provisions for which a direct charge is made. Typically these are: rents on council homes, school meals, swimming bath entrances, library fines and charges for public transport. This group represents a large income, but they are also the subject of high costs. Therefore, when we think about such revenue sources, we must think in *net* terms. Net means effectively any surpluses or profits made from the provision of these services. Sadly for most authorities they are nearly all loss-making, and therefore are not sources but drains on revenue. Certainly most housing and transport authorities run, unavoidably, at a loss.

Nevertheless, we do add some of these fees as separate (though small) revenue streams which make some contribution to local finances. It is also important to consider that they represent possible future opportunities for growth. In the modern era of commercial style operations in government, every possible source of income must be considered. Thus such proposals as charges for entry to libraries or large parks, and even top-up contributions to school resources by wealthier parents are being considered.

At the moment this is a relatively insignificant contribution to local funds, but it may become an increasingly important feature if there are further squeezes on local government revenue.

Borrowing

Virtually all borrowing takes place in order to finance larger, one-off capital projects. Examples include school buildings, housing, road developments, council offices or plant and machinery. Just as most families have to borrow to spread the costs of buying a home or a car, so too do local authorities. There are three sources of borrowing:

- private banks
- the general public, in the form of local authority securities which can be purchased by individuals and firms in return for regular interest payments
- central government which operates the Public Works Loan Board.

Of course it must be remembered that all such borrowings must be paid for in the future, in the form of both regular interest charges and the repayments of the capital sum itself. Therefore it should be seen as a benefit to the current residents, which must be paid for by future taxpayers. Fortunately, since the projects concerned normally carry a long-term benefit, those who pay will also enjoy those benefits.

At first sight this seems to be both a great opportunity and also a hazard for local authorities. It represents a potentially unlimited source of funds as well as a danger that they may run up debts which will become unsustainable. But the power to borrow is not like a credit card with no spending limit. There are strict controls exercised by central government. These take three main forms:

1 The Public Works Loan Board gives each local authority a credit allocation. If it wishes to borrow above this limit, the high interest payments charged act as a powerful deterrent.
2 Most large capital building and transport developments require the approval of the relevant government minister. Since such projects are normally financed from borrowing, the minister has effective control over credit by controlling the spending for which it is to be used.
3 Since the Local Government and Housing Act 1989, every local authority has an effective credit limit. If it exceeds this, financial penalties may be applied.

Sale of assets

This has proved to be a controversial element in local revenue. There have been two main sources of such funds:

1 There has been a large income from the sale of council homes to their tenants since the Housing Act 1980.

2 Councils have developed a system of selling assets, mainly office buildings, to property companies. This provides a large cash boost for the authority, and the asset is then leased back (ie rented) from the property company.

The effect is very much like borrowing. An instant cash inflow is paid for over many future years of annual payments. Like borrowing, it appears to be an almost unlimited source of income, but also like borrowing, central government has been careful to avoid uncontrolled spending. Most of the funds from such asset sales can only be used to repay past debts. The rest can be used for new spending projects, but the amount is limited. Only 25 per cent of housing sales revenue and 50 per cent of other receipts may be used for general spending purposes.

European Union Funds

Local authorities may apply for European funding (largely from its Regional Fund) for large scale projects which will enhance the economic and environmental development of a region. These funds are only available where the national government cannot supply them. In 1997, for example, Huddersfield obtained £2.4 million from the EU for the redevelopment of its historic city centre, a project it could not have undertaken from its own resources.

Since such schemes are normally regional in nature, it is necessary for groups of authorities to cooperate in applying for grants (as we shall see below, this is a strong argument for the future development of regional government). Typically they concern transport, water conservation, environmental protection, forestry and economic development schemes.

Lottery Funds

This is one of the most recent sources of revenue. It is normal for voluntary, private organisations to apply for funds in conjunction with local authorities. Characteristically these are plans in the Arts, for spending facilities and for local environmental improvement.

This is not an enormous source of funding, but it does represent an important new way in which local councillors can sponsor projects which could not have been previously considered, being of marginal interest.

Private Finance Initiatives (PFI)

This was the 'big idea' of the 1990s in the field of local government finance. Though developed by the Conservative Party, it has also been embraced enthusiastically by Labour. It is essentially a means by which large capital spending projects can be financed by a partnership of local government (possibly central too) and private enterprise.

Private firms which have large amounts of available capital to invest may be invited to put up the finance for a new project, such as a school, leisure complex, housing estate or road building programme. They will receive a set return on their investment out of the local authority's normal revenues. In some cases, the private enterprises involved may be invited to manage the development in the long term, again in return for a regular fee.

This has a number of perceived advantages:

1 It taps a large pool of investment finance which may be lying idle.
2 It provides local government with a relatively cheap source of financial capital (less expensive than bank finance, for example).
3 It involves private enterprise directly in the provision of local services and so, hopefully, creates a greater sense of community involvement; it may help to erode the strict distinction between the public and private sectors which results in lack of flexibility.
4 It suits the Labour Party's idea of a 'stakeholder society' where more people are concerned directly with the business of government.

SUMMARY OF LOCAL GOVERNMENT REVENUE

This list is now a formidable one. An inventory is therefore needed. Local authorities raise revenue in the following ways:

- **Local taxation** – Council Tax; Uniform Business Rate; precepts.
- **Central government grants** – specific grants; Revenue Support Grant; Challenge Funding.
- **Fees and charges** – profits from running services, rents and other charges.
- **Borrowing** – bank loans and overdrafts; issuing local authority bonds; Public Works Loans Board.
- **Other sources of capital** – European Union; National Lottery Grants; sales of housing or other assets; Private Finance Initiative.

It is small wonder, then, that councillors spend almost as much of their time considering how to raise money as they do in deciding on expenditure!

The proportion of total revenue accounted for by each of the above categories is shown in the diagram opposite. The key figures concern the balance between locally generated revenue and that which is controlled by central government. In the figures shown, less than 20 per cent of all revenues are accounted for by methods which are in the control of the local authority (Council Tax and some other miscellaneous sources). We can say that about 80 per cent of local government revenue is directly in the hands of central government ministers.

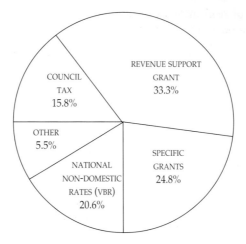

SOURCES OF LOCAL GOVERNMENT REVENUE IN ENGLAND AND WALES 1997–8

EXPENDITURE

You will no doubt be relieved to learn that the expenditure side of the local government finance equation is a good deal simpler than the revenue side. Of course the effects of expenditure are vital since they represent the actual services and developments which directly affect communities. But the calculations are much clearer. There is one key distinction between *capital* and *current* expenditure.

CAPITAL EXPENDITURE

From time to time we all have to make larger purchases which cannot be financed from our normal weekly or monthly income. Not many of us can purchase a car, a stereo system or a washing machine without making special arrangements to raise the necessary funds. Fortunately such items do not recur regularly. Once we have purchased them we can enjoy the benefits for many years before a replacement is needed. In order to pay for them, we must either use money we have saved, possibly sell something valuable which we have, but most likely we will borrow the money through a loan, a hire purchase agreement, an overdraft or through a credit card which we will pay off later. Though they are not commonly known by the name these are household *capital purchases*.

Exactly the same principle is true for local authorities (and any other organisation for that matter). Capital expenditures are usually large, too large to be funded from existing cash balances, but, once made, create long-term benefits. Local authorities rarely have sufficient cash saved to finance capital expenditure, so most of the money is borrowed. The only difference to the household situation is the availability of funds from the Private Finance Initiative, the EU or even the National Lottery Board which are described above.

Typical examples of local government capital expenditure are:

- school buildings
- leisure or sporting facilities
- road building schemes
- housing developments
- environmental improvement schemes.

Councillors are generally keen on capital expenditure projects. They make an immediate and noticeable impact and act as a long-term testimony to their work. However, there are pitfalls. These projects must be paid for in the future and can be a burden on taxpayers for years to come. They require future maintenance, which is an annual addition to future current expenditure.

Central government is generally less enthusiastic. It is not necessary to be an economist to understand that borrowing funds may have an inflationary effect. When funds which are previously lying idle – in banks, people's savings or private companies' coffers – are brought into active use, there is an effective boost in the flow of money in the economy which causes prices to rise. So, as explored below, central government ministers, especially the Chancellor, are often anxious to hold back capital spending.

CURRENT EXPENDITURE

Current expenditure involves smaller but regular demands on local government finance. They have to be funded out of the normal flow of income coming from taxes, central government grants and so on. Some of the main items are:

- wages of employees
- maintenance of plant and buildings
- housing and road repairs
- materials for schools, care of the elderly
- fees to firms operating on behalf of the council
- costs of administration of services
- rents paid to companies for use of property
- consumable materials such as fuel, stationery
- interest payments and capital repayments of past loans
- costs of council publicity
- payments and expenses to councillors.

The main feature which can be identified here is that much current expenditure is simply unavoidable. Teachers have to be paid, roads maintained, the elderly cared for and social workers despatched to help families in need. Whereas a good

the cat (central government ministers) continually attempted to capture the mouse (local government financial independence). But every time the cat found a way of catching the mouse, the mouse found a way of escaping. Unlike the end of all Tom and Jerry cartoons, however, the cat did eventually come out on top. The story looks like this:

The Grant Related Expenditure Assessment (GREA)

Introduced in 1980, the development of the GREA marked the greatest change in the financial relationship between central and local government since the nineteenth century. Before the new system, the grants (then known as the Rate Support Grant) were a matter of negotiation between ministers in London and local authorities. Each authority put in a bid for its needs for the next year. This would be justified by an extensive description of those requirements. Ministers (in reality, civil servants on their behalf) then instituted a negotiation procedure based on these estimates. The result was an agreement between the two sides. There was an appeals procedure for authorities who were still not satisfied.

Many commentators have described this system as a *partnership model*, which suggests a fairly equal relationship between the two levels. This is possibly an exaggeration, as central government still held the purse strings. But it must also be stressed that, if a local authority was dissatisfied with its annual financial settlement, it had a relatively free hand in raising local taxes or other sources of revenue to make up the difference.

The Local Government Planning and Land Act 1980 changed this in two ways:

- The assessment of a local authority's needs was now determined by ministers and civil servants in London, largely at the Department of the Environment. In other words, local authorities no longer determined their own needs. It cannot be stressed too much what a radical change this was. It removed a vital pillar of local self-government and independence. Though it was clearly an attempt to curb extravagant local spending and to provide a degree of uniformity throughout the country in the quality of services, it had the effect of shifting the balance of power decisively to the centre.
- In the past, some councils had spent more than the agreed level of expenditure by finding alternative sources of revenue. This was foreseen and the Act included a system of penalties for overspending. The formal assessment was a benchmark. If it was exceeded, an authority faced a reduction in its following year's grant, roughly by the amount of the overspend. In 1981 the rules were further tightened, especially in Scotland where overspending was rife. It was thought that this would be a sufficient discipline for authorities to conform to the assessments. This proved to be a false hope.

Supplementary rates

Some councils, notably in Scotland, showed further defiance by raising an extra tax in the course of the year to make up for reductions in the grant. These so-called supplementary rates were outlawed in 1982 under the Local Government Finance Act.

Rate capping

Scotland remained a centre of trouble when councils were determined to make up their grant penalties (some had no central government grant left at all!) by levying progressively higher local taxes (then known as the rates). The response was two Acts – the Local Government Planning Act 1982 in Scotland, followed by the similar Rates Act 1984 in England and Wales. This legislation gave ministers the power to place a 'cap' on proposed rises in the rates: when a council proposed spending too far above the annual GREA assessment, it would be forbidden from increasing the rates to make up the difference.

The introduction of rate capping ranks in importance almost alongside the 1980 Act which had established central assessment of needs. It marked a further major shift in the balance of power to London. It caused great resentment among councillors who felt their last vestige of independence was being removed, and continues to do so. They were, after all, elected and so had a mandate to carry out expenditures according to their manifestos.

Asset sales

A further loophole remained: authorities felt they could use the proceeds of asset sales to top up their sinking budgets. In order to stop this occurring, the use of asset sales for general purposes was limited to 50 per cent in 1989. It had already been stipulated in the Housing Act 1980 that proceeds from housing sales could mostly only be used to pay off past debts. Now frustrated councillors were sitting on growing bank accounts, swelled from asset sales which could not be spent. But the government held its ground.

Uniform Business Rate

At the same time as the introduction of the Poll Tax (see below), the government took the opportunity to deal with another small but nagging source of local independence. Local authorities still exercised control over the level of rates levied on commercial premises. This was another possibility for councillors to try to obtain more revenues. Jacking up commercial rates was always a problematic device since it would discourage local businesses and so have a seriously detrimental effect on the local economy. Although few councils were willing to jeopardise employment opportunities in this way, it was still a gap the government wished to fill.

The Uniform Business Rate was a system where *all* commercial premises rates level were set for the whole country (there were variations for Scotland, England and Wales). Such decisions were, therefore, taken out of the hands of local authorities.

The Poll Tax

All students of modern British politics should know the story of the **Poll Tax**, or **Community Charge**, to give it its correct name. (Apart from one famous occasion in the House of Commons, Margaret Thatcher never used the term 'Poll Tax' in public.) It contains many lessons about the nature of decision-making in the Thatcher years, about the power of pressure groups, the rule of law, the conduct of both Houses of Parliament and, of course, was a central feature in the downfall of Mrs Thatcher in 1990. Here we are especially concerned with its relationship to local government, for it is part of the cat and mouse tale which we have been recounting.

As we have seen, successive Conservative ministers had tried and failed to bring local government spending, and therefore taxation, under full control. Prime Minister Thatcher tried one more throw of the dice. Introduced in 1989 in Scotland (1990 elsewhere), the Poll Tax was an attempt to make councillors financially accountable to their electorates, a piece of the jigsaw which had always been missing.

THE POLL TAX RIOTS, 1989

The problem with the old rates system was that it was a property tax borne solely by those individuals who actually *owned* homes (tenants might have had rates incorporated in their rents, but were never directly aware of what they were paying in the form of tax). This meant that, on average, only between 25–30 per cent of the electorate actually paid the rates directly. In other words, over 70 per cent of the voters were not conscious of paying local tax at all! Why, therefore, should they not elect and re-elect councillors who consistently went in for high spending and high local taxes? This meant that the discipline of the electorate was very lightweight. The Poll Tax was to be different.

This charge was to be paid by virtually *all* adult voters. Most of the electorate would therefore have a vested interest in electing councillors committed to keeping expenditure and taxation down. It was the most subtle, but potentially the most effective scheme devised by the cat to catch the mouse. Would it have worked? The question is in the conditional tense, of course, because the tax was never properly implemented. Within three years of its introduction in Scotland it was repealed by John Major and replaced by the less controversial Council Tax.

The problem for the Poll Tax was essentially the same as its attraction to the government. It brought into the tax net many millions of new payers. This seemed logical since we consume local services as individuals, not just as households. It also spread the tax load more evenly. The old rates had been paid mainly by property owners (incidentally usually the staunchest of Conservative supporters); Poll Tax was to be paid by all. However, the army of new taxpayers, many of whom were in lower income groups, hated this extra financial burden. Above all it was not related to income so, as it was said at the time, a duke paid the same as a dustman. In hindsight, therefore, its demise was almost inevitable.

There is slight proof which suggests that the Poll Tax might have worked for the government. In the only full set of local elections to be held while the tax was in force (1991), there was a trend showing some swing away from support for those councillors who had levied higher than average poll tax levels. It was not a powerful movement, but Mrs Thatcher remained adamant that, in time, it would have grown in effect. In the event it did not matter and we shall never know.

Central government victory

Despite the poll tax debacle, the cumulative effect of all these curbs was having a powerful effect by the 1990s. The number of councils which had to be capped steadily fell. By 1997–8, 88 per cent of English and Welsh authorities were setting budgets within the Standard Spending Assessment (essentially the same as the GREA). Of the rest, only three had produced budgets high enough above the assessment to warrant charge capping (the new name for rate capping). By the end of the century local authority spending seems at last to be under control. Yet this has been at some cost to local democracy and independence.

Before passing on to the current situation we should review the important measures which have been used since 1979: see table 14.

Table 14: *Measures used by government since 1979*		
YEAR	LEGISLATION	EFFECT
1980	Local Government Planning and and Land Act	Replaced many specific grants by a block grant Established the Grant Related Assessment Instituted penalties for overspending councils
1982	Local Government Finance Act	Outlawed levying of supplementary rates
1982	Local Government Planning (Scotland) Act	Introduced rate capping on high taxing councils in Scotland
1984	Rates Act	As above in England and Wales
1988	Local Government Finance Act	Introduced the Poll Tax Introduced the Uniform Business Rate

THE CURRENT PICTURE

The position reached by 1997 was of a bewildering range of financial restraints exercised by Whitehall over Town Halls. At this stage, therefore, a summary of these controls is needed to clarify the position. The following description concerns both capital and current accounts of local authorities:

- **Capital spending** above a minimum level require the approval of the relevant government minister.
- **Borrowing** has to be similarly sanctioned. The Public Works Loans Board may levy punitively high interest rates.
- **Asset sales** can only be partially used to finance new spending. The rest is reserved for repayments of debts.
- The **Standard Spending Assessment** (formerly GREA) creates a spending straitjacket on the current account.
- **Grant penalties** are incurred by councils which overspend.
- **Charge capping** prevents excessive increases in local taxation.
- **Uniform Business Rate** controls the level of rates on commercial properties.
- The **Housing Act 1989** prevents local authorities from diverting resources from other uses to subsidise housing rents.
- General **legislation** establishes minimum standards of service. This effectively fixes a lower limit on spending on many provisions.
- The **Audit Commission** may criticise councils which do not conform to the three principles of value-for-money, which are 'economy, efficiency and effectiveness'.

There are a number of other more technical limitations which ministers can impose but the list shown above covers the main points. We must now ask what room for financial manoeuvre is left to local councillors? The answer is very little. They can be identified as:

- A little flexibility in switching expenditure from one service to another.
- Using savings through greater efficiency or contracting out services to finance other schemes.
- Some limited ability to borrow or use proceeds of asset sales for additional plans.
- Applying for, and using EU or Lottery grants.
- Applying for Challenge Funding from central government.
- Levying new charges for services in order to improve quality of provision.
- Making profits from the provision of services for which a charge is already made.

It is difficult to quantify the precise sums involved in such flexibility, but one thing is certain; the opportunities for councillors to govern their own finances are severely limited.

PROSPECTS UNDER LABOUR

Although the Labour Party has long bemoaned the lack of financial independence of local government in Britain, there are few concrete proposals which seem likely to make fundamental changes. On coming to power, Labour's intentions appeared to centre upon the following possibilities:

- Consideration of freeing the Uniform Business Rate, allowing individual local authorities to vary the rate on commercial premises.
- The possibility of local referenda to determine whether there is support for increased local taxes in order to fund improved services.
- The prospect (though distant) that charge capping may be phased out in the future. This will depend upon the success of attempts to improve the financial accountability of councillors.
- The replacement of Compulsory Competitive Tendering by 'Best Value'. The details are shown below in Chapter 4, but the effect can be described as allowing authorities to provide services of good quality rather than merely at the cheapest rate possible.
- The release of accumulated funds from the sale of assets which have in the past been reserved for debt repayments. A start was made in 1997 when £5 billion of such funds was released by the Chancellor.
- The intention to shift the balance between central government grants and local taxation towards the latter. If more local revenue comes from such taxation, it is assumed this will increase local independence.

A warning is needed here. The list shown above appears radical, but it remains largely a set of broad policy intentions and no more. The words of Hilary Armstrong, the Local Government Minister seem to be relatively unenthusiastic:

> *"In terms of finance we do have clear ideas to devolve more responsibilities to local government, but it is also true that what councils spend is accounted for in central government spending totals so we can't just say, 'Do what you want'. We will keep the power to cap **in extremis** and will make it clear what the parameters are. If councils go beyond them we will come down very heavily."*
>
> New Statesman, *25.7.97*

Nevertheless, the financial settlement for local government in 1998/9 did indicate some relaxation. Poorer areas received generous standard spending assessments and the rules of Council Tax increases were relaxed. The overall effect is likely to be a significant rise in *real* spending, especially in education and social services. It remains to be seen whether this will only be a 'honeymoon' period.

SUMMARY

As we said in the introduction to this chapter, finance is central to the character of British local government. It is not the only factor which has resulted in the centralisation of power and in the loss of self-government among authorities, but it is the most important.

The battles between local and central government have largely centred upon the latter's attempts to curb spending by the former. In so doing the discretionary powers of councillors have been inexorably reduced. Little can be achieved without financial resources. Local councillors have learned this lesson the hard way, through sometimes bitter experience. The main casualty of centralised financial control is free local self-government. The principal beneficiary is uniformity of treatment. However much commentators and politicians have mourned the loss of local autonomy, it must also be remembered that taxpayers are no longer likely to be victims of high spending councils which are not properly democratically accountable to the electorate.

STUDY GUIDE

Revision Hints

It is vital to have a set of notes which include every stage in the changed financial relationships between central and local government. For each stage, be clear about why the change occurred and what its effect was.

A few financial statistics should be highlighted, illustrating the balance between locally-determined revenue and income which is controlled by central government.

A summary of financial controls is important, both for questions on finance specifically and for more general questions about central government control. You should also add some balance points, indicating ways in which local authorities can still be financially independent.

Exam Hints

The most important and common kind of question on finance asks the student to show *changes* in financial arrangements and controls; in particular the movement from the partnership model before 1979 to the current agency model which suggests that there is little local autonomy. There should be a picture of developments between 1979–97.

The issue of why finance is so important is more difficult. Here you should be able to demonstrate that you understand how the narrower issue of finance relates to the broader question of what has happened to the powers of local government. Strong answers will include examples of this relationship. A number of these are included in the chapter.

Speculation on future developments will also require some perspective on the recent past. What has been happening? Is this trend likely to change? The extent to which Labour Party policies might suggest change or simply more of the same should be examined.

Practice Questions

1 How and why did central government increase its control over local government finance during the 1980s?
2 a Why was the Poll Tax introduced?
  b Why did it fail?

5

CENTRAL-LOCAL GOVERNMENT RELATIONS

Introduction

BRITAIN HAS NO entrenched, codified constitution. This means that the existing distribution of political power is not safeguarded. Large shifts in this balance can be achieved simply by ministers obtaining a majority in the House of Commons. The rapid and radical transfer of power away from local government into the hands of central government ministers which took place in the 1980s could, therefore, be achieved without constitutional amendments.

Indeed, it is interesting to speculate that, were Britain to feature a real constitution based on the American model for example, this change could not have occurred to the extent that it did. Constitutional safeguards which might have reserved powers to local government, just as American states retain their own sovereignty, would have made significant power transfers extremely unlikely.

As it was, the developments were not achieved without intense political controversy. In the course of those battles, rebellious councillors had to be disqualified from office, uncooperative councils were taken over by teams of civil servants and huge local authorities such as the GLC were abolished. In the end, however, one simple truth shone through. Parliament is sovereign and will, in the end, have its way; this is how it was and still is. As the new Labour administration came to power in 1997, the tide was expected to turn, but as things stand, the balance of power rests firmly in London.

"England has no local government worth the name. It has a system of local administration which is partly appointed, partly elected but even the elected element is now little more than an agent of central government."

Andrew Adonis, The Observer, *20.7.97.*

Many other commentators would agree and extend the analysis to the other parts of Britain. This chapter will examine how this has come about, after describing the permanent features which have characterised local–central relations.

Key Points

This chapter contains material on the following key issues:

- The general nature of the relationship between central government institutions and local authorities.
- How this relationship has changed over the past 20 years.
- The changing role of local government in general, especially the change from being a provider of services to a general manager of services provided by others.
- How relationships and roles may change under a Labour administration.

FINANCIAL RELATIONS

The permanent and changing features of the financial position have already been described in Chapter 3. If you have not yet studied that material, you should do so now. Finance is fundamental to the issue; it cannot be understood without such knowledge.

A few salient points do, however, bear repeating:

- Between 1979–1992, local government moved from having control over about 60 per cent of its revenue, to less than 20 per cent.
- Central government ministers have discretionary powers to veto capital spending projects, borrowing and excessive local tax rises proposed by local authorities.
- Local authorities have little flexibility in how they use their financial resources in both capital and current spending.
- The assessment of local financial needs is determined by central government. Local authorities have little opportunity to influence these assessments.
- Councillors who seek to defy the financial controls imposed on them may face surcharges (ie fines), disqualification or other financial penalties.

PARLIAMENT AND LEGISLATION

Britain is a unitary state and Parliament is sovereign. In effect, this means that what ultimately happens in local government is in the hands of any government able to command a majority in Parliament. In practice, this can involve a large variety of forms of control. Parliament can:

- determine the structure of local government boundaries. Though currently recommended by the independent Local Government Commission, the final decision is made first by ministers and then by parliament as a whole
- create or abolish new authorities. Most famously this was done when the GLC and six other city–region authorities were abolished in 1986
- prescribe certain compulsory features in the internal workings of councils. In particular, this means the mandatory establishment of various committees
- control the terms under which councillors hold office, including payments and a number of restrictions on other activities
- require authorities to provide certain services, eg education, social services, planning and care of the long term mentally ill (Care in the Community)
- lay down the minimum standards to be met in the provision of those services, notably in police and emergency services and education
- forbid councils from undertaking various activities such as commercial trading or agreeing special arrangements with foreign states
- approve or overrule by-laws made by local councils
- grant powers to ministers and other public bodies to make orders concerning the operation of local authorities.

This final feature, the granting of power to make secondary or delegated legislation, is perhaps the most controversial as it involves discretionary powers which are relatively uncontrolled. As we have seen above, this has important financial consequences, especially where rate capping and budget setting are concerned.

MINISTERIAL CONTROL

We have already seen that there are now extensive financial restraints which can be exercised by ministers and their department. These include the ability to veto borrowing, increases in Council Tax and capital spending projects. Clearly these do not merely impact upon money. They may also be of political significance. Ministers may ask what the borrowing is for, and what is the purpose of the capital expenditure. In areas such as transport, housing or education, *policy* as well as finance may be at stake.

In addition, legislation usually contains elements which give discretionary powers to ministers in other areas. So, for example, decisions on schooling, asset sales, major planning projects, transport arrangements and policing can be imposed upon councils from Whitehall. There is, therefore, a constant toing and froing between London and localities by officers who are negotiating their councils' plans, ministers, and officials in government departments.

POLITICAL INFLUENCE

It is not always the case that compulsion is needed in order to implement government policy at local level. Furthermore, it must be remembered that many councils are controlled by councillors who are members of the same party as that which controls central government. Certainly during the 1980s the Conservative government's policy of restraint on public expenditure was enthusiastically embraced by a number of councils. Westminster and Wandsworth were especially cherished by Margaret Thatcher for their efforts in this regard. Similarly, in the 1970s, Labour-controlled councils were devoted supporters of the spread of comprehensive education. Much of this programme was accomplished without the need for legislation or compulsion of any kind.

A variety of methods may be used to explain government policy to local authorities and to make clear what is required. The most common, however, is the **circular**. This is really an instruction, although it may be couched in friendlier terms. The implication behind all of these is that if compliance is not forthcoming, more robust means are likely to follow.

INSPECTION

A number of bodies exist, mostly independent of government, who check the work of local authorities. Four of these should attract our special attention:

THE AUDIT COMMISSION

In overall terms, the Commission may make general comments about the way in which local government finance is being handled, including comments on efficiency. However, such reports do not refer to individual authorities. Here the work is left to district auditors, who look at the financial affairs of every council every year.

They are looking for fraud and corruption of course, but on a political level it is expenditure which is most important. Auditors will be aware of the legal limitations on local spending. Should any expenditure be outside these limits, there may be serious consequences. The most celebrated example of their work came in 1985 when councillors in Liverpool and Lambeth were disqualified from office for proposing excessive spending which would have had the effect of bankrupting their council.

Auditors have increasingly been prepared to highlight examples of inefficiency, wastefulness and wilful overspending. The auditors' reports which highlight such problems may then be used by ministers and Parliament to bring councils back into line. Where an immediate legal remedy is possible, the courts may also be used to correct the financial irregularity in question.

THE OFFICE FOR STANDARDS IN EDUCATION (OFSTED)

This body inspects all educational establishments, most of which lie under local government control. In extreme circumstances such as Calderdale in 1996–7, they may even inspect the whole local education authority where there is a suspicion that it may not be upholding high standards in education.

On the whole, however, OFSTED is concerned with the performance of local education advisers, whole schools, governors, head teachers and teaching staff. OFSTED reports recommend action for improvement and, in extreme circumstances, may urge staff changes or dismissals.

It has potentially wide powers, illustrated in September 1997 when Hackney Education Authority was effectively taken over by the Inspectorate on the grounds that it was failing in its duty to provide a satisfactory standard of education in the borough.

THE PARLIAMENTARY COMMISSIONERS FOR LOCAL GOVERNMENT (OMBUDSPERSONS)

Three exist in England and Wales, with equivalents in Northern Ireland and Scotland. Technically they are employed by Parliament and they certainly report to a select committee. In practice, however, they work on behalf of members of the public.

Ombudspersons, as they are commonly known, investigate cases of maladministration by local authorities. Typically this will concern undue delay in dealing with applications for planning consent, social care or repairs. In addition they may be critical of unequal treatment of people by officers or poor service quality which results in loss or distress.

They cannot order compensation or other remedies themselves, but a critical report usually does result in an authority putting right the wrong they have done to an individual. Where a common type of problem seems to arise continually, ombudspersons may recommend ministerial intervention or even legislation.

THE CITIZENS' CHARTER

Introduced by Prime Minister Major in the early 1990s, the Citizens' Charter sets minimum standards of performance for a number of public bodies including local government. Thus local authorities are expected to publish their achievements in such fields as transport, road repairs, social services and inspections. Where these fall below published standards, they may attract the attention of ministers but above all, run the risk of losing the support of the electorate.

Though not strictly a part of the Charter, the publication of league tables of school performance in Standard Attainment Targets, GCSEs, A Levels and other qualifications is part of the same principle; that the public should be made aware of the performance of public bodies, and that these should reach a pre-determined minimum level. They provide a discipline which was seen to be lacking in bodies which had been insufficiently accountable to the public in the past.

COMPULSORY COMPETITIVE TENDERING AND 'BEST VALUE'

COMPULSORY COMPETITIVE TENDERING

In attempting to make any government body more efficient, one fundamental problem stands in the way. Unlike commercial organisations, public bodies are not normally required to make profits. On the whole, they do not sell services directly and so the normal economic test of performance – by how much does revenue exceed costs? – cannot apply. Therefore, the question is asked, how do we judge performance? And against what standards?

Of course targets can be set, as we have seen above through the Citizens' Charter, but these are artificial and arbitrary. An idea arose in the 1980s, however, which has partially solved the problem. This is known as Compulsory Competitive Tendering (CCT). Under the Local Government Act 1988 a number of local government services were specified as suitable for CCT. The example which has become familiar is refuse collection. Under CCT the service must be put out to tender to private firms who then compete with each other to be granted a contract. Competition is based on a combination of lowest cost and satisfactory quality. The local authority's own workforce is also allowed to tender for the service as if it were a private company.

The resulting contract is granted to the best bid (normally the cheapest, but only if quality is guaranteed). In this way the local authority *must* prove that it can operate successfully along sound commercial lines if it is to retain control of the service. Where the contract is awarded to private enterprise, the community gets the most efficient service and, hopefully, best value for money. Sadly for them, the management and workers employed by the local authority lose out in such circumstances (though many council workers have been re-employed by winning private contractors, often at lower wages).

Since 1988 the number of services which *must* be subject to CCT has steadily increased and includes such functions as house and road repairs, maintenance of parks and gardens, environmental planning, school meals and a variety of social service roles.

BEST VALUE

The Labour Party has been suspicious of CCT since its introduction in 1988. They have seen it as a means of forcing workers to accept extremely low wages so that their employers can secure contracts. It is also thought to create job insecurity, unwanted bureaucracy and open up possibilities for corruption in the awarding of contracts. Nevertheless it has also been supportive of the principle of value for money in local government. On coming to power in 1997, therefore, Labour sought an alternative, which appeared in the form of '**Best Value**'.

The concept has been described by Geoffrey Filkin, a former local authority chief executive, in this way:

"Best value asks of every service; could it change and be more efficient? Do other authorities or service suppliers manage to deliver more to the public? If they do, a council that is committed to the public will either use these other means of service delivery or will ensure that its own efficiency and quality are raised rapidly to the same standard."

Geoffrey Filkin. *Best Value to the Public.*
Discussion paper for The Municipal Journal 1997

In other words, local authorities will no longer be *forced* to offer services out to competitive tender, but will be *required* to demonstrate that they are successfully combining efficiency and quality. This can be achieved by any means which works. Some services will be run by local authorities themselves, others by private enterprise. It may be that authorities will cooperate to provide services jointly.

The key question is the manner in which central government will enforce Best Value. The Audit Commission will play a leading role undoubtedly, but the criteria against which good practice will be judged or benchmarked is yet to be determined. Thirty local authorities in England, Wales and Scotland have begun a pilot scheme in the spring of 1998, with full implementation to follow in the year 2000.

THE CHANGING ROLE OF LOCAL GOVERNMENT

"If the previous [Conservative] government did have anything that amounted to a coherent policy towards local government, it was to by-pass councils wherever possible and accumulate more power for the centre"

Steve Richards, New Statesman, *25.7.97*

Other commentators such as Professor John Stewart have characterised the role of local government since 1980 as enablers rather than providers of services to the community. In fact there is now a near unanimous verdict among experts that local authorities have lost their key role in service provision and are now responsible for a relatively narrow range of functions, with little discretionary power.

We need to ask, therefore, two questions:

- Where has all the power gone?
- What is the true role of local government at the end of the twentieth century?

LOSS OF FUNCTIONS

Since 1980, local authority services have endured a veritable onslaught of legislation and government initiatives which have had the effect of significantly reducing their role. Responsibility for the lost services have gone in two directions, as shown in the diagram below: Essentially they have moved either upwards to central government departments or to quangos and other bodies appointed by those departments, or downwards to lower tier authorities or to voluntary bodies. In order to illustrate we can use three services as examples of this process, as in table 15.

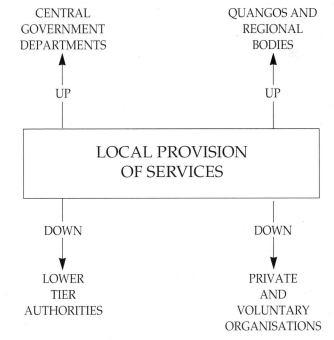

CENTRAL GOVERNMENT DEPARTMENTS

QUANGOS AND REGIONAL BODIES

UP   UP

LOCAL PROVISION OF SERVICES

DOWN   DOWN

LOWER TIER AUTHORITIES

PRIVATE AND VOLUNTARY ORGANISATIONS

WHERE HAVE LOCAL SERVICES GONE?

Table 15: *Three local authority services showing loss of function*	
EDUCATION	
DEVOLVED DOWNWARDS	TRANSFERRED UPWARDS
• Local management of schools gave control over school budgets to head teachers and governing bodies • Parents given more say on governing bodies • Parents given greater freedom to choose schools for their children with an appeals system to handle grievances • Inner London Education Authority dissolved in central London. Functions transferred to individual London boroughs	• Schools allowed to opt out of local authority and become 'grant maintained' under control of the Education Department • Schools obliged to follow the National Curriculum controlled by an education quango, the School Curriculum and Assessment Authority (SCAA) • Standard Attainment Targets for 7–16 year-olds established by SCAA • Higher Education Colleges and Polytechnics taken out of local authority control. Transferred to Education Department and a funding quango, the Further Education Funding Council

HOUSING	
DEVOLVED DOWNWARDS	TRANSFERRED UPWARDS
• Councils forced to offer council homes for sale to tenants ('right to buy legislation') • Council tenants allowed to opt to transfer to voluntary housing • Increased government funding to private housing associations • Contacts for housing repairs to be offered to private sector through CCT	• Increased funding for house building through the government-appointed Housing Corporation rather than through local authorities • Ministers empowered to exert greater control over level of council rents • Housing Action Trusts (HATS) set up by government to manage low-cost housing estates

PUBLIC TRANSPORT	
DEVOLVED DOWNWARDS	TRANSFERRED UPWARDS
• Councils forced to open public transport services to private contractors • Local authority transport services forced to submit to CCT on main routes	• Department of Transport took over control over licensing of public transport • London Transport transferred to government-appointed quango, London Passenger Transport Authority • Similar arrangements to London made in other metropolitan areas

This has left relatively little for local authorities to manage! Similar processes have occurred in such roles as police, urban development, road maintenance and environmental services.

It should also be stressed that the traffic has not all been one-way. Local authorities have been asked to take on extra responsibilities. For example, the Children Act 1989 increased their responsibility for the protection of children in special need. Similarly, the Care in the Community programme transferred care of the long-term mentally ill from the National Health Service to local government. However, these certainly do not balance the losses of function elsewhere. In addition, the additional functions are considered to be 'Cinderella' services, those which are not considered glamorous, have special difficulties and are not wanted by other bodies.

THE MODERN ROLE OF LOCAL GOVERNMENT

It is still true that local authorities are providers of services. They do have a role in running schools; they remain responsible for children's welfare, for care of the elderly and the long-term mentally ill. They still repair roads and houses and look after parks, gardens and libraries. However, it is questionable whether that providing role is their *principal* function any more. Most commentators suggest it is not.

Instead, local authorities are usually seen as enablers or facilitators of services, which is what recent governments have wanted them to become. What does enabling mean? We can identify a number of features of this role:

- Awarding contracts to private and voluntary organisations for the provision of services.
- Ensuring that the terms of such contracts are met.
- Inspecting the performance of other organisations which operate in the community.
- Coordinating the work done in the locality by a variety of quangos and other organisations, which are not directly under local authority control.
- Making joint arrangements with central and regional bodies.
- Representing the interests of the community to central government, to quangos and to other funding bodies such as the EU.
- Representing the views of members of the community in how services are to be run, thus seeking to ensure sensitivity to local needs.

Rather than providing, we should think of such activities as overseeing, inspecting, coordinating and managing. They are still key functions, but very different in character to the pre-1979 circumstances.

SUMMARY

The changes in the role of local government and the enormous transfer of power away from local level to central government and its appointed quangos in the last quarter of the twentieth century have been considerable. Indeed, there is some justification for suggesting that they have been the most important political and constitutional changes experienced in Britain for over 100 years.

Simon Jenkins has suggested that this has been one – the most significant – part of a process of nationalisation of the governing process. He suggests that this has taken place at a time when local democracy in the West has actually been growing. In his words,

> *"Historically it was British local councils that led the way in their independence, indeed insularity, from central government. They formed the template for civic democracy in the United States, from the eighteenth century to this day, and used to be contrasted with, say, France and Spain. Since 1980 Britain has moved in the opposite direction from the rest of the world."*
>
> *Simon Jenkins,* Accountable to None, Penguin, 1996

So, if Jenkins is right, something extraordinary has happened. A less radical view would accept that there has been some adjustment in the balance of power in the direction of central government, but this does not yet constitute the complete demise of local autonomy.

STUDY GUIDE

As in the previous chapter, it is important to create a file of all the key controls which have been introduced since 1980. These should be added to and dovetailed with the financial changes described above. This will give a clear pattern of *change*.

There must be a clear evidence, including examples, of how the role of local government has changed as a result of legislation and ministerial interventions. You should have a clear picture of what constitutes providing services and what is meant by the enabling function.

There should also be a set of reasons listed which explain why this has taken place. Once again the financial factors should be placed alongside the political changes.

Exam hints

There are three main categories of question here. They can be characterised as, Why? What? and With what result? You should be prepared to explain why these changes took place – what was the political background? The nature of the changed relationship will have to be described in some detail. Finally a picture of what the situation was by 1997 should be drawn; What was the role of local government at that time?

Of course, as with all analytical questions, there must be some balance added. The remaining autonomy of local authorities should be expressed, and some assessment of the extent of the change attempted.

Finally, a view of future developments may be required. To what extent are changes under Labour, such as elected mayors, devolution and the restoration of metropolitan authorities, likely to restore some degree of independence to local government? On the other hand, the process of centralisation may prove to be long-term and not susceptible to political change in Westminster.

Practice Questions

1 Discuss the view that local authorities are now little more than agents of central government control.
2 In what ways has the relationship between central and local government changed since 1979? Why did these changes take place?
3 What is meant by the observation that local government has changed from a provider of services to a mere enabling authority?

6

LOCAL DEMOCRACY

Introduction

THE MARKED CENTRALISATION of powers in Britain and the loss of local authority autonomy are part of a wider debate about the current state of local democracy. The balance of opinion in this debate suggests two concerns: first, that democracy in local government has been in decline for several decades, and secondly, that this is an undesirable development and needs to be reversed.

It would be wrong to suggest that this view is unanimous. It has been pointed out, usually in Conservative Party circles, that excessive local autonomy and popular control can lead to unwanted ends. Examples have included:

- Overspending by councillors anxious to retain popularity among service consumers.
- Considerable variations in the standard of services offered.
- Projects undertaken in the interests of vociferous minorities rather than the community as a whole.

But this is largely a hangover from the 1960s and 70s. In the two decades since the heyday of local government, most of these problems have been dealt with. The issue in the 1990s asks the question of whether the reduction in local independence may have gone too far. Professor Vernon Bogdanor has expressed such a view:

Whatever the intentions, centralisation has proved conducive neither to accountability nor effective government. Instead it has given rise to a democratic deficit.

Vernon Bogdanor, New Statesman, 25.7.97

We may now explore the nature of this 'democratic deficit' to which Bogdanor refers.

THE DEMOCRATIC DEFICIT

This has a number of elements, as follows:

- Turnouts at local elections remain stubbornly low. Compared to about 75 per cent at general elections to Parliament, local elections normally have a 30–50 per cent electorate turnout. Part of the reason for this is thought to be apathy, but it is also suggested that voters recognise the relative impotence of local government and so see voting as worthless.
- There has been a significant transfer of functions to quangos and to large joint boards which are not elected, and so are not seen as democratically accountable.
- There is a lack of identifiable leadership in local authorities. Unlike central government, local authorities have no government or cabinet as such. This also means that there is no local head of government. Although there are leaders of councils, they do not have the same authority or power as prime ministers. The effect is a lack of focus for the electorate, and it is difficult to pinpoint who is accountable for what decisions.
- Too many local authorities are under single party control and so there is a lack of effective opposition and accountability.

There are some positive elements, of course. Local pressure groups proliferate and are demanding a voice and some influence; there is a vigorous and well funded local press which can inform the public; councils are now required to offer more information to the community. But serious concerns remain. Study of the institutions of local democracy illustrates further the current state of local democracy.

LOCAL ELECTIONS

THE SYSTEM

(The following description of how elections work does not apply to Northern Ireland; the situation in the province is described separately below.)

The system used for local elections is far from clear. It varies according to the type of authority, and is further complicated by the fact that authorities of the same type may not conform to the same pattern. It is therefore necessary to make certain generalisations. The following features can be identified:

- There are fixed terms between elections. The period varies, but the principle is always the same – each authority has standard terms. By-elections take place where a councillor dies or retires, but otherwise all local elections take place on a specified date in May.

- The electoral system is first-past-the-post as in general elections. As we shall see, Northern Ireland uses a proportional system, but in the rest of Britain, the candidate or candidates who receive the most votes are simply elected.
- In general, councils may choose whether the whole council is elected every four years, *or* whether one third of the council is elected every two years. This gives rise to a rather confusing set of elections each year, with some *whole* councils being up for re-election, some *thirds* of councils, and some authorities where no election is scheduled at all.
- In all parts of the country, councillors represent an area known either as a ward or a division. These vary considerably in size so that there may be one, two or three councillors representing each area.

The striking feature of this system is its sheer complication, and there is little doubt that confusion over when and where local elections are taking place adds to low turnout and apathy. The Widdicombe Committee recommended simplification, suggesting common election dates for all councils and smaller single-member divisions and wards. However, there is little likelihood of such a reorganisation until the structural reforms of the Local Government Commission are completed.

A description of the nature of local elections for the years 1994–7 is shown in table 16, illustrating the complex nature of the system.

VOTING

Apart from low turnouts and the complexity of the system which confuses voters, the principal problem of voting at local polls is that the electors tend to vote on *national* rather than *local* issues. Evidence to the Widdicombe Committee in 1985–6 suggested that about 80 per cent of voters support exactly the same party in local elections as they do in general elections. Widdicombe found this inconclusive. In one sense, the idea that 20 per cent of voters *do* discern between local and national issues may be seen as impressive. On the other hand, it must be dispiriting for local representatives to feel that, no matter how frugal they may be, however well they organise services, their chances of re-election depend largely on the performance of their national colleagues at Westminster.

A striking example of this effect occurred in the period between 1992–7 when the Conservative Party lost huge numbers of seats in local government. In 1996, for example, the party lost 573 out of the 1091 it had held among those seats being contested – over a half! In 1995, they lost 1768 out of the 3834 which they contested. These losses were largely due to the extreme unpopularity of the government in London. It seems impossible that such huge reverses could have been due to widespread poor performance by Conservative councillors.

Table 16: *Local elections 1994–7*				
YEAR	TYPES OF COUNCIL	NO. OF COUNCILS	PROPORTION ELECTED	FEATURES
1994	English Metropolitan districts County districts Welsh districts Scottish regions & islands London Boroughs	36 114 4 12 32	Third Third Third All All	Marked Conservative losses and Liberal Democrat gains
1995	English Metropolitan Districts English County Districts English and Welsh new unitary authorities	36 274 36	Third Some thirds, some all All	Huge losses for the Conservatives and gains for Labour. Many independents lost seats
1996	Northern Ireland Districts English Metropolitan Districts English Unitary Authorities	26 100 14	All Third All (with 1 exception)	Poor showing for Sinn Fein in N.Ireland. In England, Labour and Lib Dem gains at the expense of the Conservatives
1997	English Counties English Unitary Authorities	34 17	All All	Elections held on the same day as General Election so a high turnout. A small Conservative recovery

Some degree of voter independence does, however, exist. The principal beneficiaries have been the Liberal Democrats. In 1995–7, the Liberal Democrat share of the vote in local elections held up at about 25 per cent, during a period when their showing in national public opinion polls languished at 15–20 per cent. In particular, the party enjoys a disproportionate quantity of local support in South West England and in Scotland. Most poignantly, when the local elections took place on the same day as the General Election in 1997, the Liberal Democrats achieved a much better local result than in the national contest, suggesting that many voters actually 'split the ticket' on the same occasion. Rallings and Thraser for example, report marked turnrounds in Liberal Democrat fortunes in Cambridge and Pendle.

PROPORTIONAL REPRESENTATION (PR) AND NORTHERN IRELAND

The system for local government (and EU) elections in Northern Ireland is known as **Single Transferable Vote (STV)**. This is a form of proportional representation. It is beyond the scope of this book to describe all the characteristics of PR, so that only a brief description of STV is offered here. In essence, each local constituency returns a number of councillors rather than just one. Voters are presented with a number of candidates from each party, together with some individuals who are independents or representatives of very small groups.

The voter places candidates in order of preference. He or she may select candidates from different parties and may show any order of preference. Voters may also mix their preferences between independents and party representatives. The result is that the various parties gain seats more directly *in proportion* to the votes cast. The first-past-the-post system which operates elsewhere in Britain tends to distort voting strengths, and makes it more likely that the large parties will win seats at the expense of the smaller ones. In other words, the seats are not awarded in proportion to voting strengths.

Why is a more proportional system used in Northern Ireland? As you may have guessed, it is the unusual political situation which makes this system so desirable. Without STV, it is likely that the candidates from Unionist parties would gain a disproportionately high number of seats. This was one of the grievances which led to unrest after 1968.

By awarding seats in almost direct proportion to party strengths, all sections of the community may feel they gain a fair share of representation.

We can see the implications of this by reviewing the 1996 local elections in table 17. Seats are awarded on a more or less proportional basis, and a wide variety of groups are represented. Whether this could have a successful application elsewhere is discussed below.

Table 17: *Northern Ireland local elections 1996*		
PARTY	PERCENTAGE OF VOTE	SEATS WON
Ulster Unionist	24	30
Social Democratic Labour Party	21	21
Democratic Unionist	19	24
Sinn Fein	15	17
Alliance Party	7	7
UK Unionist Party	4	3
Progressive Unionists	3	2
Ulster Democratic Party	2	2
Northern Ireland Women's Conference	1	2
Labour Party	1	2
Others	2	0

SOURCE: KEESING'S UK RECORD 1996

THE GROWTH OF QUANGOS

Since the 1970s there has been a steady process whereby functions of local authorities have been transferred to quangos (also known as Non-Departmental Public Bodies – NDPBs), which are by their nature unelected and unaccountable. Before proceeding, some examples are required to illustrate this development:

1 **Regional Transport Executives** were set up following the abolition of the GLC and six other metropolitan councils. They are staffed by a mixture of councillors delegated from lower tier authorities and central government nominees. They are expected to control public transport and traffic management in urban regions.
2 **Housing Action Trusts** began to replace the council provision of housing in certain areas in the early 1990s. Members were appointed by central government and they were funded by a combination of public and private funds.
3 **Training and Enterprise Councils (TECS)** contain representatives from both the public and private sector. They exist to provide educational and training opportunities for young people not served by the conventional educational system.
4 **Urban Development Corporations** channel central government and private funds into inner city regeneration projects, a function formerly handled exclusively by local authorities.

The members of this 'quangocracy' have been described by Professor John Stewart as the **New Magistracy** in the sense that they have tremendous influence over local affairs and yet are virtually completely unaccountable. The **Nolan Committee** on conduct in public life, which was first reported in 1995, also expressed concern over the way in which such bodies were appointed and the dangers inherent in the lack of democratic control over them. Nolan recommended a more open and politically balanced system of appointments, but stopped short of suggesting elections to such bodies. We will return to this theme in the next chapter on regional government issues.

LOCAL ACCOUNTABILITY

THE PROBLEMS

The difficulties associated with local elections impact predominantly upon local accountability. But they are not the only difficulty. The lack of accountability has, for many years, been an intractable problem. We can identify six reasons why it has proved so difficult:

1 Low turnouts at elections mean that usually over half the voters do not bother to demonstrate their opinion on the performance of councillors in the most direct manner available to them.

2 The concentration on national issues even in local elections means that the actions and effectiveness of councillors are likely to have little impact upon their chances of being re-elected.

3 There is widespread ignorance about local government. Even those who vote may have little knowledge of the council's work, and will be unlikely to know how the parties' *local* policies differ.

4 Many voters are not directly responsible for paying the Council Tax. These non-payers, therefore, do not have a vested interest in the financial behaviour of their council.

5 Since local government is perceived to be relatively impotent today, voters may understandably feel that they are unable to hold councillors accountable, since they are not themselves responsible for much of what the council does.

6 Many councils have been, and are likely to continue to be, under the continuous control of the same party for many years. This is especially true of urban authorities which are governed by Labour. The danger in this situation is that councillors of the ruling party, confident in the knowledge that they are virtually guaranteed re-election, feel no pressure to be publicly accountable.

SOLUTIONS?

Remedies for lack of local accountability have proved frustratingly difficult to find. Indeed, as we have seen, the attempt through the Poll Tax led partly to the demise of Margaret Thatcher as Prime Minister. What is particularly striking about the types of solutions described below, is their wide variety. This suggests both the complexity of the problem and the difficulty in finding answers.

The Widdicombe Report

This placed the responsibility squarely in the hands of parties. Though the committee was suspicious of the influence of party groups, it also recognised that party domination of the electoral process was both inevitable and desirable. It was felt that only parties could present coherent policies, provide the necessary publicity for the electorate and create genuine competition for public office. However attractive non-political local government may seem, it will not provide accountability, so parties must be in the front line.

However, some specific reports were proposed in 1986 by the committee. In particular it suggested simplification of elections and the imposition of smaller local constituencies so that each councillor should represent a manageable size of community. Critics have seen this as mere tinkering, and certainly no real progress has been made as result of the report.

The Poll Tax

As we have seen above, this was an attempt to make more people subject to local taxation so that they would be sensitive to the financial conduct of councillors. However, the attempt at its introduction was a failure and there is little prospect that future tax reform will deal with the issue.

The Citizens' Charter

The introduction of this and similar devices such as school examination league tables, has had an interesting effect. Councils do now provide more information to the community about their services and level of performance. Voters therefore have more information upon which to base their voting intentions.

Elected Mayors

If introduced, this reform may help. Theoretically, such elected officials could provide a focus for accountability which is lacking in the current system. There are difficulties, however. Such mayors could not be like prime ministers who can dominate policy-making. There is no guarantee that mayors would come from the same party as that which controls the council (if indeed any single party is in power). It would clearly not be acceptable to make mayors responsible for the work of the council if they do not also have the power to control it.

Community Plans

These may provide a new initiative. Brighton and Hove council, for example, have pioneered a system whereby members of the community are presented with the options open to the authority in the governance of the locality, and invited to make comments on how they can best be served. The plan (published under the title 'Help us Shape the Future') includes the expenditure implications of various services, so that a financial judgement can be made by respondents. In this way the council may discover what people think about its performance, and also establish the priorities in services which the community values.

Brighton and Hove's plan corresponds with a general Labour Party policy to give more information to the public about local government's work and to create systems of feedback. These include ideas for local referenda on spending and taxation proposals, panels of electors who would be consulted regularly, and more extensive market research about services.

Proportional Representation

This would probably loosen the control of larger parties and introduce more independents and representatives of small groups such as the Green Party. Indeed, very few councils would be under single party control as the election results would be more proportional. The impact on accountability is uncertain, but it could be argued that less party control equals greater public control. The experience of Northern Ireland and the future assemblies in Scotland and Wales where PR will be used, may result in its introduction for local elections on mainland Britain.

THE FUTURE

It would be wrong to suggest that dramatic progress is being made in this area. However, there is some room for optimism that local government can become more accountable to the public for what it does and how it does it. Indeed, Steven Bassam, leader of Brighton and Hove Council which is at the forefront of reform has expressed such hopes:

"I know these are hard times financially, but there are great times ahead so long as we don't resort to trench warfare."

The Guardian, *13.8.97*

But if Bassam's optimism proves to be a false dawn, we may have to rely upon central government ministers and MPs in Parliament to make local government accountable on our behalf.

COUNCILLORS AND CONSTITUENTS

The relationship between a local councillor and his or her constituents bears a marked similarity to that between Westminster MPs and their electorates. Indeed councillors, like MPs, have often remarked (and sometimes complained) that they have become little more than social workers.

Though we may imagine that councillors spend most of their official life in council and committee meetings, this is not true for many. Rather, they are concerned with the everyday problems of constituents in their relationship with the council and other public bodies. The addresses and telephone numbers of councillors must be publicly available (mainly through public libraries), so that they are constantly accessible to members of the community.

Typically, they try to solve difficulties of housing, planning applications, social services provision, educational issues and local road or traffic arrangements. They act as an interface with the officers who run the day-to-day affairs of the authority. In so doing, of course, they also gain information about what constituents want.

Less directly, councillors often also join voluntary bodies in the community. These usually include community health councils, school governing bodies, environmental pressure groups, tenants' organisations, housing associations or chambers of commerce. In this way, they maintain a permanent regular contact with the community.

Unlike the position regarding accountability, therefore, local democracy does seem to be in a healthy state in this regard. The hearing and redress of individual grievances, a feature described by Professor Philip Norton as 'tension release', is a key element in a strong democracy. On the whole, local government fulfils this requirement.

PRESSURE GROUPS

Possibly the most striking example of active, pluralist local democracy is to be found in the United States. This is not the result of high voting turnouts (sometimes as low as 15 per cent), but rather of the proliferation of pressure groups which operate at this micro level there. As long ago as 1830, the French philosopher Alexis de Tocqueville noted how vital this was in America in cushioning individuals against the threatening power of the central state. While such a grand claim may be difficult to sustain in Britain today, it is nevertheless true that local pressure group activity may be the principal way in which many individuals actively participate in politics.

The Widdicombe Committee noted an increasing trend towards interest group activity in the 1980s, and saw it as a healthy development. Until members of the public began to take their own action in this way, there was a danger that local government would fall into the hands of local élites controlled by political parties, business groups or trade unions. Widdicombe suggested that the spread of interest groups was reducing such a danger.

Interest groups operate on three basic levels:

- Members have gained representation on council committees and other official bodies, a kind of local **corporatism**. In this way they may have a direct influence on authority decision-making.
- Councillors may become members of these groups and so provide a two-way flow of information and influence between the community and the council.
- Interest and pressure groups help to mobilise public opinion and so are able to influence the authority.

Who and what are these groups? A definitive list of such groups would be extremely long, but a shorter selection may serve to illustrate the range of interests which are concerned. This is shown in table 18 on p. 88.

THE COUNCIL OF EUROPE CHARTER OF LOCAL SELF-GOVERNMENT

This was signed by the new Labour government on June 3 1997, barely a month after taking office. The Charter, which came into existence in 1985 under the

Table 18: *Pressure groups*	
TYPE OF GROUP	TYPICAL ACTIVITIES
Chambers of Commerce	Represent the interests of local traders and businesses
Tenants Associations	Press the council to maintain and improve housing provision and policing provision
Environment groups	Campaign for better local environment through traffic measures, improved parks and gardens and controls over local industry
Friends of Parks	Seek better provision of parks and other recreational facilities
Parents' Associations	Place pressure on the authority to improve educational provision
Minority groups	Press the authority to provide facilities or grants to minority groups and to provide protection where they suffer violence or discrimination
Arts groups	Seek funds and facilities for local arts projects

auspices of the Council of Europe and its 40 member countries, is designed to ensure that its signatories 'protect and develop the rights of local authorities'.

The fact that the new Labour government was so quick to sign up to such a declaration certainly suggests a strong commitment to local democracy. Hilary Armstrong, the British minister who signed on the country's behalf, added a clear statement of intent:

> *"Let us examine ways in which we can develop pilot studies on a wide range of issues — best value, a new approach to regeneration, community planning and partnership with other agencies, and democratic innovations."*
>
> Presswire, 5.6.97

She also criticised 'ritualistic gatherings of ministers and local government', describing them as 'pointless affairs'. These were certainly fine words and good intentions. However, concrete measures must follow if her intentions are to bear real fruit.

SUMMARY

At a time when attempts are under way to democratise the institutions of central government, there are still serious concerns that, at local level, democratic principles remain weak. As we have seen, these issues have a variety of aspects. They can be summarised as follows:

- Accountability is weak. Elections do not satisfactorily serve their main purpose of forcing elected councillors to be truly responsible for their actions.
- Local elections in general are unsatisfactory with low turnouts (always a scourge of unhealthy democracies), local issues not being properly covered during campaigns, and too often parties winning because of the performance of central government rather than that of councillors.
- There is still widespread ignorance and apathy about the role and operation of local government among the public.
- Where a single party controls a council, especially when this has occurred over a long period of time, there is a danger that representatives are insufficiently sensitive to popular opinion.
- Many functions which were previously the responsibility of councils, and therefore subject to accountability, have been transferred to unelected, unresponsible quangos.

However, there are encouraging signs. The Labour government's support for local self-government through the Council of Europe demonstrates a commitment to local democracy. Authorities are beginning to recognise that they must serve the public more effectively and must provide more information about their work. A number of proposals by central government, such as elected mayors, reductions in the functions of quangos and experiments in testing local opinion about local government are likely to emerge. Above all, there is a greater recognition that councillors and officers serve the public rather than their direct political masters. It cannot be said that the wind of democracy is blowing through the corridors of local government, but a strong breeze has certainly sprung up.

Revision Hints

It is essential to list the ways in which democracy appears to have suffered in recent years, but you must balance this against areas in which democratic controls and principles still flourish. Note the characteristics of local elections, along with possible proposals for reform and the likely effects of such changes.

The issue of accountability is crucial. Note the ways in which accountability is weak, but also ways in which councillors can continue to be made responsible for their actions. There should be a catalogue of attempts which have been made, and which are proposed in the future to remedy this aspect of the democratic deficit.

In all cases, illustrations should be selected to demonstrate the nature of these problems and their solutions. Aspects of local government elections and the conclusions of the Widdicombe Committee would be especially useful.

Exam Hints

The most common kind of examination question suggests that local democracy is either dead or dying, and asks you to examine this proposition critically. Clearly a description of what is implied by the term 'democracy' is needed, especially in a local context. Answers should reflect, as usual, change which has occurred in modern times. What developments have caused the decline of democracy, and in what ways? There should be some balance, suggesting that there are ways in which local democracy still flourishes. An assessment should reach a firm conclusion as to the current state of democracy and may make some speculative remarks about future prospects.

More specific tasks may concern the characteristics of elections, and a critical assessment of their operation should be prepared for. The same is true of the principle of accountability itself. The issue of how accountable local government is and how it could be made more so should be contemplated. In both cases, include recent and prospective changes in any answer.

Practice Questions

1 In what ways has local democracy been in decline in recent years?
2 a Why is turnout so low in local elections?
   b What steps could be taken to revitalise local democracy?
3 a What factors determine the results of local elections?
   b Does it make any significant difference which parties win local elections?

7

DEVOLUTION AND REGIONAL GOVERNMENT

Introduction

IN SEPTEMBER 1997, the voters of both Scotland and Wales demonstrated their support for the setting up of devolved assemblies and governments in their countries. At the same time, efforts continue to find a political settlement in Northern Ireland which may result in devolved government there too.

Turning to England and its distinctive regions, the picture remains cloudy. Some degree of consensus exists between the Labour and Liberal Democrat parties that more regional autonomy is desirable in the English regions, but the political will, either among the people or the politicians, may not prove to be strong enough to bring the issue through to fruition.

The meaning of the term **devolution** is described in Chapter 1 and in the glossary, but we should remind ourselves at this stage of what the process entails. It is certainly a transfer of considerable amounts of political power to a region, but stops short of granting complete **legal sovereignty**. It implies the establishment of both an elected assembly and an executive to govern that region, but the devolved government remains under the jurisdiction of the British Head of State, ie the Monarch. Devolution may be extensive, as will occur in Scotland, or modest, as in Wales. Finally we must emphasise that taxation powers may or may not be transferred under devolution.

In the next four sections we will limit our discussion to Scotland and Wales, but there then follows a consideration of the prospects for devolution as part of a new settlement for Northern Ireland.

Key Points

This chapter contains material on the following key issues:

- The nature of devolution in principle.
- The background to the devolution issue in Scotland, Wales and Northern Ireland, including the referenda of 1997.
- The various arguments which have been advanced in favour of and against devolution.
- The arrangements which have to be made for the implementation of devolution.

FOR OR AGAINST DEVOLUTION?

THE CASE FOR DEVOLUTION

In this chapter we will find many political and economic causes for the transfer of powers to Cardiff and Edinburgh. But we need to search more deeply to find the profound sources of devolution demands. Why should these national regions develop such a clear desire to break some of their ties with England?

If we pose a series of questions, an answer may ultimately emerge:

- Is there a distinctive culture which is considered to be under threat from domination by a generally British or specifically English way of life?
- Are there significant differences in living standards which might lead to discontent within the region?
- Has the economy of the region its own specific features to the extent that it requires a separate set of industrial and commercial policies?
- Does the region have its own distinct institutions which need to come under separate democratic control?
- Are there marked differences between the region and the rest of Britain in attitudes towards the running of such services as education, health, social services and local government provisions?
- Does the region have its own specific transport, planning and environmental problems which need to be dealt with independently?
- Is there a significant degree of discontent with centralised political control, and is this discontent unable to find sufficient legitimate, legal outlets for its expression under current arrangements?

If the answer to these questions is *predominantly* 'yes', then there would appear to be a strong case for devolution to that part of the United Kingdom.

THE CASE AGAINST DEVOLUTION

It is true by definition that if there is an insufficiently strong case for devolution made out, based on the criteria listed above, it can be argued that there should be no change. The less crucial problems can often be dealt with *within the current political structure*, in other words through reform rather than transformation. This is the classic Conservative position, sometimes characterised by the colloquial expression, 'if it ain't broke, don't fix it'. A more conventional version of the principle might be that Conservatives prefer to 'change what is bad and retain what is good'.

Indeed, in the past, gradualism has been the approach adopted whenever Welsh or Scottish discontent has emerged. A separate Scottish Office was established in 1885 to satisfy demands for administrative devolution. The Office was given greater status in 1926 and its powers have been steadily increased as the need has arisen. A similar arrangement has followed in Wales. Here, however, fears over the loss of the Welsh language have caused most disquiet. Legislation to guarantee its use in schools, law courts and administrative institutions was the successful response.

So opponents of devolution will argue that it is simply not necessary; there *are* alternatives. Yet there are also more serious objections which can be raised. These suggest that the consequences of devolution will be undesirable. The clearest of these are listed:

- It will add a further layer of government in the political system. This will cause excessive bureaucracy, lead to further confusion over who is responsible for which services, and be expensive to run.
- It will lead to constant disputes between the devolved government and central government in London. However clearly the demarcation line over responsibilities is drawn, there is bound to be an overlap, which will create damaging conflict and delays. This will be especially problematic if different parties are in control in London, Edinburgh and Wales.
- Some suggest that Scotland and Wales (or Northern Ireland for that matter) are simply too small to run their own affairs fully. This is particularly true of economic development which requires support from the great resources available to British government as a whole. There are fears that they will rapidly become severely deprived regions.
- The Labour Party currently dominates voting in both general and local elections in Scotland and Wales. Should this continue in Scottish and Welsh assembly elections, it could be that both countries will experience one party control for the foreseeable future. This, critics argue, will lead to a loss of democratic accountability which has dogged local government in many regions (especially in Scotland).
- Above all perhaps, opponents fear that devolution will be the first step on the path to the disintegration of the United Kingdom. Given a taste of autonomy, they suggest, the Scots and the Welsh will create irresistible pressure to be granted full independence. The end of the British Union would be, for these critics, an absolute evil.

Ironically it is a Labour MP, Tam Dalyell, rather than a Conservative, who perhaps expresses most eloquently this greatest apprehension:

> *The [devolution] proposals are indeed the beginning of a motorway without exit to a separate Scottish state.*
>
> *Tam Dalyell*, The Observer, *24.8.97*

MODERN ORIGINS OF DEVOLUTION

There have been political movements campaigning for complete or partial independence in Scotland and Wales ever since they became part of the United Kingdom. In the case of Wales this dates back to the early middle ages, but in Scotland the Act of Union of 1707 is the starting point. Wales has never really enjoyed full independent statehood. Indeed, as a properly united country, it has always been subject to rule by English monarchs. Scotland, on the other hand had its own king until 1603 when James I of England (VI of Scotland) united the two thrones, and its own Parliament with legislative powers until 1707. But this is not a history book so we must seek more recent developments.

The modern debate on devolution begins in the late 1960s. This period saw a revival in the issue and in the fortunes of both the Scottish and Welsh Nationalist parties (the latter is called **Plaid Cymru**, which means the Party for Wales). Why did this occur? Four principal causes have been commonly identified:

1 At that period, the relative decline in the state of the British economy, in comparison with her principal competitors, became more distinct. The sterling crisis of 1967 (the external value of the pound collapsed and British trade was severely threatened) brought matters to a head. In both Scotland and Wales there was a sense of betrayal, that the unsuccessful running of the economy originated in London. The Scots and the Welsh felt that their economies remained fundamentally healthy.

As part of that same process, traditional industries such as coal, steel and shipbuilding were in decline. Wales and Scotland, where there was concentration of these industries, felt the full force of these developments. Naturally there was a hope that, given the opportunity to run their own economies, they could do better than the English.

2 Politically the process of centralisation of government was becoming apparent. Local government everywhere was beginning to lose its independence and there was an increase in the degree of state control over industry and commerce. Though the geographical distance between London and Edinburgh or Cardiff is not great, the political gap seemed to be widening.

3 With the growth of broadcasting and other media, especially of television, there was a growing fear that specifically English culture was beginning to dominate at the expense of traditions which used to flourish around the fringes of the British Isles. This was particularly felt in Wales where the domestic language was under increasing threat.

4 A specifically Scottish phenomenon was the commercial exploitation of North Sea oil in the mid-1970s. The oil crisis which followed the Arab-Israeli war of 1973 and led to a quadrupling of world crude oil prices in 1974–5, had a dramatic result. The huge oil fields under the North Sea off the coast of Scotland had hitherto been too expensive to exploit successfully. With higher world prices, however, the North Sea reserves became enormously attractive and serious drilling commenced.

To many Scots, these oil reserves were rightfully theirs, but most of the benefits (in the form of highly lucrative petroleum revenue tax which oil companies pay) were enjoyed by England. There naturally followed a campaign to repatriate the benefits of North Sea oil to Scotland, and this strengthened nationalistic feelings.

The upsurge in interest in greater autonomy for Wales and Scotland was reflected in the General Election of October 1974. There was a modest but distinct increase in support for the three parties which supported some form of devolution, ie, the nationalists and the Liberals. Table 19 shows their electoral support at that time. This placed the issue of devolution firmly at the forefront of the political agenda of the 1970s.

PARTY	SEATS WON	PERCENTAGE VOTE
Liberal	27	18.3
Scottish Nationalist	11	30.4*
Plaid Cymru	3	11.1*

Table 19: *Some results from the October 1974 General Election*

*PERCENTAGE OF VOTES IN SCOTLAND AND WALES ONLY

THE EVENTS OF 1978–9

During 1974 it became apparent to the Labour Party that it ought to reflect the growing interest in the devolution issue. It was especially important as Scotland and Wales provided them with a strong concentration of electoral support. Without winning the vast majority of seats in the two countries, Labour could not hope to win a general election and form a government. The fact, therefore, that the Party decided to include support for devolution in their manifesto of October 1974 could be seen simply as a cynical attempt to win votes.

It was certainly true that the Party was not united behind the policy although, in their defence, there was a majority in favour. As we shall see, the lack of sufficient political will within the Party may have been the ultimate cause of the failure of the policy.

By 1978, Labour had lost its slender House of Commons majority owing to a number of by-election losses (when the Party had taken power in October 1974, it only had an overall majority of three). It now relied upon the support of Liberals and Nationalists to win controversial votes and so stay in office. The price the government had to pay was to push through its lukewarm proposals for devolution. So, a rather reluctant Party was forced to draw up legislation in 1978. The Scotland and Wales Acts were introduced and found majority support in the Commons. However, a major snag emerged.

It had always been understood that devolution would only occur if there were referenda held in the two countries and that the majority of the people showed their support. At first sight this made Welsh devolution unlikely as there was undoubtedly insufficient public support, but also made Scottish reform a strong probability. At this point, the government's weak position let it down. An amendment to the referendum proposals was tabled. This required that, not only a majority of *those who voted* should be in favour, but that a total of at least 40 per cent of the *total electorate*, including those who did not vote, should approve. With a relatively low turnout expected, the 40 per cent rule looked to be a serious impediment. The government opposed the amendment but two Labour rebels defied the leadership and supported the proposal. This was enough to carry it. This subsequently proved to be the death sentence both for devolution and, ultimately, the life of the government itself.

The result of the referenda which were held early in 1979 are shown in table 20. A narrow vote in favour in Scotland fell foul of the 40 per cent rule, while in Wales, as expected, there was insufficient support by any measurement.

Table 20: *Result of referenda in 1979*		
DEVOLUTION REFERENDA, 1979	PERCENTAGE OF TOTAL VOTING IN SUPPORT	PERCENTAGE OF TOTAL ELECTORATE IN SUPPORT
Scotland	51.6	32.9
Wales	20.3	11.9

The proposals now lay in ruins and were abandoned. Inevitably Labour lost the support of its smaller allies in the Commons and a vote of no confidence soon followed. The defeated government resigned in May of that year and lost the resulting General Election. Labour was relegated to opposition for the next 18 years.

THE ISSUE RE-EMERGES

On 1 May 1997, not a single Conservative MP was elected in either Scotland or Wales. No table of statistics is required to illustrate such a stark result. Of course much of this catastrophe for the Tories was the result of a tired, discredited government failing to deal with its apparently low standards in public life, its internal divisions over Europe and a variety of other political difficulties. Yet the party's implacable opposition to devolution in either Wales or Scotland played a significant part. How had this come about? For the answer we must return back to the beginning of the Conservative administration.

After 1979, interest in devolution had briefly waned. The economic success of the government in the boom years of the mid 1980s deflected interest away from the issue. When recession struck at the end of the 1980s, however, the devolution debate reared its head again.

As in the 1970s, economic failure was blamed on London politicians. The process of political centralisation which had begun 20 years before gathered pace again. In addition there was a growing gap between living standards in the South of England and the rest of the country (the so-called North–South divide). In 1995, the average standard of living in Scotland was 3 per cent below the average for the whole of the UK, while in Wales the average individual earned about 18 per cent below the national average. Scotland and Wales thus felt the effects particularly keenly and resented it.

As in 1974 when North Sea oil provided an extra fillip to the supporters of autonomy in Scotland, the late 1980s also saw key incidents which excited interest in the issue. At that time the government announced a programme of coal mine closures which effectively spelled the end of Wales' traditional central position in the industry. It was not just a blow to her economy, but also to her culture which had been attached to coal for over two centuries. It was seen as London's unwillingness to show support for Wales' industrial base.

In Scotland it was the Poll Tax which caused the trouble. It was decided to introduce the tax one year earlier in Scotland, in 1989 instead of 1990, than in the rest of Britain. Not only did most Scots hate the tax *per se*, they also saw themselves as being used as guinea pigs in an experiment in local taxation.

During the 1990s, Labour watched and noted the growing discontent. It is interesting to note that Labour had had three successive leaders who represented Welsh seats – Callaghan, Foot and Kinnock – and their two successors were both Scots – Smith and Blair. There was, therefore, a strong non-English tradition in the upper echelons of the party. It was ultimately John Smith and Tony Blair who insisted that the party should adopt devolution as a central feature of its proposals for constitutional reform.

There was a different atmosphere to the 1979 situation too. Now the Labour Party was almost totally united behind the policy. Opinion polls were also suggesting that legislation, and the referenda necessary to underpin it, would gain an easier passage this time. The election of a Labour government in 1997 with a huge Commons majority set the scene for a successful devolution campaign.

SCOTTISH DEVOLUTION

SCOTTISH NATIONALISM

Whatever economic and social reasons we can find behind the modern demand for devolved government, it must always be remembered that it is the upsurge in Scottish nationalism which has been the decisive factor. What is its nature?

To some extent, it is economic in character. The Scots have long believed that they have greater potential than the rest of the United Kingdom. They emphasise the tradition of research and innovation in such fields as medicine, industry, transport and science which has long flourished in Scotland. Certainly it seems that the Scots have had an impact well beyond the size of their population. They also excel in the Arts, in sport, entertainment and intellectual life. Their achievements in these fields are almost equal of England's.

Scottish education is a source of pride, notably several first class universities with a world reputation. There is a strong industrial and transport infrastructure in Scotland, with a number of well-established industries such as steel, motors, engineering and agriculture. All this means that the Scots feel they have the potential to be economically successful on their own. Nationalists recognise this and desire the chance to realise their potential.

Scottish culture is not under serious threat from England and it would be a mistake to believe that this is an important element in nationalism there. The Gaelic language has long since ceased to be used and there is no great distinction between the cultural life of Scotland and the rest of Northern Britain. The tartan and the bagpipes may give the appearance of distinctiveness, but they are superficial elements in a way of life which remains essentially British.

So Scottish nationalists are mainly suggesting that their country has great potential which has been inhibited by their close associations with England. Devolution or independence for them will have the effect of releasing the energies and creativity of a superior society.

THE POSITION BEFORE 2000

The devolution of power to Scotland will not, in fact, be quite as dramatic as might appear to be the case at first sight. Remember that a considerable amount of *administrative* devolution has been in place in Scotland as far back as 1885. In addition the country has long enjoyed its own separate, distinct institutions and, although the Westminster Parliament was responsible for all laws, most legislation remained in the hands of Scottish MPs. The distinctive nature of Scottish politics can be summarised as follows:

- Scotland has its own official Church – the Church of Scotland. It also issues its own bank notes through the Bank of Scotland, though their value remains tied to the pound issued in London. Most sports are governed by separate national bodies and the Arts scene is very distinct from the rest of Britain, notably as a result of the existence of the Scottish Arts Council.
- The education system is separate from that of England and Wales, being controlled by the Scottish Office in Edinburgh. In particular there are different public examinations in force and the universities are self-governing.
- Scotland has its own laws. Although both civil and criminal laws are promulgated in the Westminster Parliament, a different set of laws applies in the country. There are not vast differences, but there are some important distinctions: eg, it is easier for people under 18 to marry there; the system for the transfer of property ownership differs from England and Wales; and it is possible for criminal trial juries to bring in three rather than two verdicts. In addition to 'guilty' and 'not guilty', a Scottish jury may free a defendant on the grounds that a case is 'not proven' (they think s/he may be guilty but there is insufficient proof). Non-controversial laws are normally handled in Parliament by the Scottish Grand Committee, an assembly of MPs who sit for Scottish constituencies only. This does leave a particular bone of contention – that disputed laws are still passed by *all* MPs, so that English or Welsh members may vote on issues which do not affect their own countries at all.
- There is a separate legal system administered by the Lord Advocate and the Solicitor General for Scotland. This has meant that the court structure is different to the rest of Britain and that there are distinctive arrangements for the conduct of criminal investigations and of trials or cases in general.
- The Scottish Office, located in Edinburgh and largely staffed by Scottish civil servants, has a great degree of independence over the administration of and public expenditure on such areas of responsibility as health care, transport, environmental protection, planning, water supply, housing, local government in general and industrial development.
- There is a wide variety of quangos which are responsible for many aspects of Scottish life. These range from the highly specialised Deer Commission, to key institutions such as the Law Commission for Scotland, the Scottish Economic Council, three Water Authorities and the Scottish Tourist Board. The White paper on Scottish devolution (Cm 3658) of 1997 identified a total of 37 executive agencies, 33 advisory bodies, and 25 other public bodies which deal specifically with Scotland and will come under the control of a new Scottish Executive after 2000.

So we see a picture of a country which already enjoys a considerable degree of autonomy. Because of this, the changeover to devolved government may not be excessively complicated. The independent legal system is already in place so little need be done with the judicial branch of government. There is already an executive branch in the shape of the Scottish Office so a bureaucracy is ready to take over smoothly. It is mainly the legislature, the new Scottish Assembly, which will require the most upheaval.

THE SCOTTISH REFERENDUM

Held on 11 September 1997, the referendum asked two questions:

1 Do you want a devolved Scottish Parliament and Executive in accordance with the government's proposals?
2 Do you want the Scottish Parliament to have the power to vary the level of income tax in Scotland by up to 3 per cent up or down?

The results are shown in table 21.

<table>
<tr><td colspan="5" align="center">**Table 21:** *Referendum on Scottish Devolution, 11.9.97*</td></tr>
<tr><td>QUESTION</td><td>NUMBER IN FAVOUR</td><td>PERCENTAGE IN FAVOUR</td><td>NUMBER AGAINST</td><td>PERCENTAGE AGAINST</td></tr>
<tr><td>Do you want a Scottish Parliament established?</td><td>1,775,045</td><td>74.3</td><td>614,000</td><td>25.7</td></tr>
<tr><td>Do you want a Scottish Parliament to have tax varying powers?</td><td>1,512,889</td><td>63.5</td><td>870,263</td><td>36.5</td></tr>
<tr><td colspan="5">Turnout: 61.5% of total electorate</td></tr>
</table>

Though not legally binding on Parliament, the positive referendum result made it inevitable that legislation would be passed to establish devolved power in Scotland.

THE DIVISION OF RESPONSIBILITIES AFTER 2000

As a result of devolution the functions of government will be divided between London and Edinburgh. Table 22 indicates which responsibilities will remain with central government and Parliament and which will be transferred to Scotland. As we have seen above, many of these functions were in the hands of the Scottish Office before devolution, but it remains an impressive list of changes.

Table 22: *Division of responsibilities after 2000*	
FUNCTIONS RESERVED TO CENTRAL GOVERNMENT	FUNCTIONS TRANSFERRED TO A DEVOLVED SCOTTISH GOVERNMENT

• The constitution of the UK
• Foreign policy
• Defence and national security
• Border controls
• Economic and financial policy
• Control over trade and commerce
• Employment law
• Social security policy
• Regulation of most professions
• Transport safety
• Other miscellaneous duties
	• Health • Criminal and
	• Education (all levels) civil law
	• Science and • Electoral
	   research funding arrangements
	• Training and • Legal system,
	   related policies police and prisons
	• Local government • Emergency services
	   operation • Liquor licensing
	• Social services • Protection of
	• Housing animals
	• Regeneration of • National heritage
	   declining areas • Environmental
	• Land use and protection
	   building control • Agriculture,
	• Economic and forestry and
	   industrial fisheries
	   development • Food standards
	• Tourism • Sport
	• Public transport • The arts
	• Waterways • Public information

THE DEVOLVED PARLIAMENT

The Scottish Parliament will have five principal functions:

1 To make laws which will apply in Scotland together with regulations necessary for the administration of the services listed above.
2 To establish powers which are to be exercised by members of the Executive and other public bodies in Scotland.
3 Approval of spending and taxation decisions made by the Executive.
4 To make the Scottish Executive publicly accountable for its decisions, including scrutiny of the work of its various departments by select committees.
5 Through the balance of party representation, it will effectively determine the composition of the Scottish Executive, including its First Minister.

The other arrangements for the Parliament will be as follows:

• There will be 129 members of the Scottish parliament (known as MSPs). Seventy-three will be elected through constituency elections on the basis of first-past-the-post. The remaining 56 MSPs will be elected through a system of proportional representation. Each registered party will draw up a list of candidates (known as 'additional members') and seats will be awarded to these members in proportion to the total votes cast for each party. So, for example, if the Liberal Democrats won 25 per cent of the total votes, they would be awarded 14 additional seats (one-quarter of the 56 available).

- It is widely assumed that the proportional element in the system makes it unlikely that any one party will win an outright majority in the assembly, so that coalition governments are likely.
- There will be a fixed term of four years for the parliament. However, the parliament may be dissolved and an election held before four years have elapsed under two circumstances – if there is no agreement on who should be First Minister, or if two-thirds of the MSPs vote for a dissolution.
- Members of Parliament in Westminster or of the European Parliament will be entitled to be Members of the Scottish Parliament simultaneously.
- A system of committees will give detailed consideration to legislation and scrutinise the work of the Executive and other public bodies.
- It will be situated in Edinburgh.

THE SCOTTISH EXECUTIVE

Following assembly elections, a First Minister (note the title 'prime minister' will not be used) must be appointed. The White Paper on Scottish devolution describes the procedure for this appointment thus:

The first Minister will head the Scottish Executive and will be appointed by the Queen on the advice of the Presiding Officer [the 'Speaker' of the Scottish assembly] after the Scottish Parliament has nominated a candidate who will normally be the leader of the party able to command a majority of support of the Scottish Parliament.

Scotland's Parliament, *Cm 3658*

This apparently simple statement disguises a potential minefield of problems. What if no single party has an overall majority? This is a likely event in view of the proportional system of elections. What if no leader can form a satisfactory coalition of parties? It is probable that, in the absence of an overall majority, the leader of the largest party will be forced to form a government. The rather chaotic scenes which often accompany attempts to form coalitions in Italy or Holland may be seen in Edinburgh in the future.

However, once a First Minister has emerged, s/he will appoint other ministers to form the Executive. Collectively they will establish policy, coordinate the work of government, establish parliamentary business, propose legislation and the budget, and control the Scottish bureaucracy and the other public bodies which will administer Scotland.

There will still be a Secretary of State for Scotland who will be a Westminster MP and a member of the British Cabinet. His or her role will be to represent the interests of Scotland in that Cabinet and act as a coordinator between the work of London and Edinburgh.

FINANCIAL ARRANGEMENTS

This is potentially the most controversial element of the new system. The key element is known as the 'Block', a sum of money allocated to Scotland. Most of the public expenditure available to Scotland will come from this Block. The only other sources of income will be the Council Tax and the Business Rate which are available to local authorities.

The sum available will be based (as it has been before devolution) on the population of the country and an assessment of needs. In the past Scotland has received on average more public expenditure per head than the rest of the UK. This was the result of a perception that the country had special problems which required some form of subsidy from more prosperous England. At one time, indeed, Scotland was receiving 16 per cent more in public expenditure per head of population than applied in England. Since 1978, however, a system has been operated, known as the **Barnett Formula** after the minister who devised it, designed to bring expenditure down to the overall UK level. This may cause potential problems if the Scots begin to suffer from significant reductions in public spending. Vital public services may begin to suffer. By 2000, the total sum involved is estimated to be £14 billion.

The Scottish Executive, with the approval of Parliament in Edinburgh, will decide how this sum is to be spent. In addition Parliament may approve an increase of up to 3 per cent in income tax paid by Scots (but no other taxes). The extra revenue raised can then be used to top up the Block grant from London. They may also *reduce* income tax by up to 3 per cent in Scotland, but this will result in less funds being available to the Executive. At current values, this represents a variation of £450 million in expenditure up or down.

There is immense potential for tension between Scotland and London in this system. Scotland will have to accept what is given. With only the solitary Secretary of State for Scotland and a small group of MPs to defend their interests, Scots may feel starved of much needed funds by English ministers. The Scottish Parliament will have little power to find alternative sources of money.

THE WEST LOTHIAN QUESTION

This issue of the **West Lothian Question** is named after the constituency of Tam Dalyell, the MP who first brought the matter to prominence, and is likely to cause a good deal of disquiet under devolution. The difficulty is as follows:

There will still be a number – probably 59 – of MPs elected in Scottish constituencies who will sit in the Westminster Parliament (remember, these will NOT be members of the Scottish Assembly). These MPs are needed to represent the people of Scotland on matters which remain the responsibility of the British government, for example, defence, foreign affairs and economic policy. So far, so good. However, these MPs will also be able to vote on issues which affect only England or Wales, such as health, social security or transport policy. This seems clearly unfair. MPs from English or Welsh constituencies will no longer have any say in specifically Scottish affairs. Why then should Scottish representatives be able to interfere outside their own country?

It had been argued that Scottish MPs in London should be disqualified from voting on English and Welsh issues. Again this does not seem to present a problem. But this is not in the interests of a Labour government. They rely on the support of such MPs who are overwhelmingly from the Labour Party. Without them, a future Labour administration may not have a majority on English and Welsh matters. The problem threatens to rumble on for some years to come.

SUMMARY

Scottish devolution is the most important constitutional development in Britain since the partition of Ireland in 1921, which brought into being the political entity of Northern Ireland. It creates a powerful Parliament which will administer the affairs of nearly four million Britons. It may, in due course, be the precursor of full independence for Scotland.

Will this be an advance for democracy? Most of those who supported the measure, including the Labour and Liberal Democrat parties together with Scottish Nationalists, say yes. However, if Scotland falls into the hands of one party government which fails to be fully accountable to the people, democracy may have taken a backward step.

It also establishes a legislature which will be elected by proportional representation. Britain will have the opportunity to witness a large scale (much bigger than that in Northern Ireland) 'experiment' in the new system. It may also be that the problems of coalition formation will be illustrated if no party can gain absolute control of the Parliament.

Most importantly, however, the principle of government by consent has been reconfirmed. The Scots gave their clear mandate to the Westminster Parliament to legislate for this vital constitutional change.

WELSH DEVOLUTION

WELSH NATIONALISM

Whereas Scottish nationalism has had a distinctly economic and intellectual basis, its Welsh counterpart is predominantly cultural in nature. In this regard it is language which plays a key role. About 20 per cent of Welsh people speak Welsh either permanently or occasionally. But it is more as a symbol of cultural defensiveness than as an end in itself, that the preservation of the language has become the central feature of the nationalist movement.

Most Welsh people understand that the country is too small and has too few of its own resources to be able to sustain a healthy economy. In 1995, the average Welsh family was 18 per cent less well off than people in the rest of the UK. Without English support, there is a real danger that Wales would become an unacceptably deprived region. For this reason nationalism is relatively moderate in nature. There are pockets of radical republicanism, especially in areas of North and West Wales where the language still flourishes. The issues which do tend to excite the interest of Welsh separatists are language, sport, the Arts and nonconformist religion. These distinctive features of their society are seen as threatened by English culture.

ALL PUBLIC SIGNS IN WALES MUST BE BILINGUAL

Thus, for the Welsh, the main value of devolution is likely to be the preservation of the culture through new democratic institutions. The language may remain a minority interest, but the Welsh have made it clear that they are determined to maintain their distinctiveness within the Kingdom.

THE GOVERNMENT AND POLITICS OF WALES BEFORE DEVOLUTION

It must be stressed that Wales has always enjoyed a lesser degree of autonomy than Scotland. In terms of administration, the government of England and Wales have always effectively been lumped together as one. This is true of education, local government, health, social security, civil and criminal law and a variety of other public services. Nevertheless there have been a modest number of national institutions to separate the principality from the rest of the UK.

The key institution is the Welsh Office which was founded in 1964. This is headed by a Secretary of State with Cabinet status. He and his office administer that part of public expenditure which is destined for services in Wales. There are also a number of large quangos in the principality, but the most important is the Welsh Development Agency. This administers a large fund available for industrial grants and incentives for foreign companies to set up in the area. The agency has had a turbulent and controversial life with accusations of patronage by the Conservative Party, inefficiency and even corruption.

Politically too, Wales has demonstrated only weak levels of independent aspiration. Plaid Cymru, the Welsh Nationalist Party, enjoys only pockets of solid support; in most of the country it trails far behind the Labour Party. The tradition of Protestant nonconformist religion (including Methodists, Baptists and Unitarians) sits more comfortably alongside socialism than nationalism. As we have seen above, the Welsh firmly rejected devolution in the 1979 referendum.

It was, therefore, surprising that Labour decided to resurrect the devolution debate in Wales in 1997. The driving force by then was not only cultural, however. There was also considerable dissatisfaction with the economic performance of the Welsh Office and the Welsh Development Agency. The Conservative Party, which is implacably opposed to devolution, won no Welsh seats in the 1997 Election. So the scene was set for a new attempt to democratise government there. In the event it proved to be a very close run affair.

THE SECOND REFERENDUM ON WELSH DEVOLUTION

This took place on 20 September, 1997. The result was extremely close, as is demonstrated by the figures shown in table 23. The initial reaction to the result was that this was an inconclusive outcome and certainly opponents of the use of referenda *in general* can find an ideal illustration of their case in this case. But the government pointed out that a majority was a majority and this was enough.

Besides, the referendum was only advisory and they had a clear electoral mandate from the General Election to introduce devolution. With its huge parliamentary majority, therefore, the Labour government was assured of the successful passage of the necessary legislation.

QUESTION	NUMBER IN FAVOUR	PERCENTAGE IN FAVOUR	NUMBER AGAINST	PERCENTAGE AGAINST
Do you want a devolved government and assembly?	559,419	50.3	552,698	49.7
Turnout: 51.2% of total electorate				

Table 23: *Referendum on Welsh Devolution, 18.9.97*

The distribution of voting in Wales was also interesting. Every district which borders on England produced a majority 'No' vote. Only Pembrokeshire in the far South-West broke the pattern. The 'Yes' vote was to be found in three distinct areas – the agricultural West, the Welsh-speaking North-West and the valley towns of the South which have suffered most from industrial decline. This demonstrates a number of instructive features:

- Language played a part, but not a decisive one, in the result.
- The proximity of England clearly weakens the sense of separate Welsh identity.
- The economic issue was a key factor in the South.

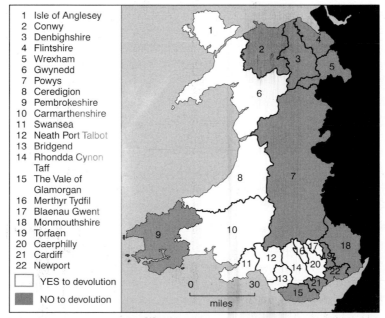

1 Isle of Anglesey
2 Conwy
3 Denbighshire
4 Flintshire
5 Wrexham
6 Gwynedd
7 Powys
8 Ceredigion
9 Pembrokeshire
10 Carmarthenshire
11 Swansea
12 Neath Port Talbot
13 Bridgend
14 Rhondda Cynon Taff
15 The Vale of Glamorgan
16 Merthyr Tydfil
17 Blaenau Gwent
18 Monmouthshire
19 Torfaen
20 Caerphilly
21 Cardiff
22 Newport
☐ YES to devolution
■ NO to devolution

HOW THE UNITARY AUTHORITIES OF WALES VOTED

But, despite this schism in Welsh opinion, devolution is going ahead. The people may have demonstrated little enthusiasm for reform, but circumstances dictate that they will get it.

THE NATURE OF DEVOLVED WELSH GOVERNMENT

The two main institutions are the Assembly and the Executive.

The Assembly

- Sixty full-time members will be elected. Forty will be returned from existing parliamentary constituencies. The other 20 will be elected from party lists in proportion to votes cast for each of those parties. Thus each person has two votes – one for a constituency MP, the other for a party.
- It will be possible to sit simultaneously for the Welsh Assembly and either for Westminster Parliament or the European Parliament.
- The Assembly will have fixed four year terms.
- There will be committees formed in the Assembly to deal in detail with the main areas of responsibility devolved to Wales. The Chairpersons of each committee will form the Executive (possibly known as a Cabinet).
- It will pass secondary (detailed) legislation, but not primary or major legislation which will remain with Parliament in London.
- It will hold the Executive to account.
- It will also exert democratic control over Welsh quangos.

The Executive

This will be drawn from the Assembly. It will be exclusively from the majority party if there is one, otherwise it will be a coalition. It will administer the allocation of public expenditure in a number of areas shown in table 25. This amounts to about £7 billion at 1997 prices.

It will also take over the work of a number of quangos which will be abolished, and will oversee the work of others, notably the Welsh Development Agency. The Executive will be accountable to the Assembly and so will be under more direct democratic control than the Welsh Office has been in the past.

The position of Secretary of State for Wales will continue to exist. His or her role will be to maintain relations between the London government and that of Wales in Cardiff. This will also retain Wales's representation in the Cabinet itself.

It is important to emphasise what the Assembly and the Executive *cannot* do, as this will demonstrate the extremely limited nature of Welsh devolution:

- There will be no separate Welsh laws.
- Welsh government will not raise any of its own taxation (with the exception of Council Tax levied by local authorities).

- It will have no power to vary the level of existing taxation.
- Though the local government structure in Wales is different to that of England, being unitary in nature, the Welsh government will not control this structure.

We can now summarise the division of powers between devolved Welsh government and that of the United Kingdom; see table 24.

Table 24: *Division of powers*		
POWERS DEVOLVED TO WALES		POWERS RESERVED TO THE UK GOVERNMENT AND PARLIAMENT
• Economic development • Agriculture • Forestry • Fisheries and food • Industrial training • Education • Local government • Health • Social services • Housing	• Environmental protection • Planning • Transport and roads • Arts • Welsh language • Sport and recreation • Historic buildings	• Foreign affairs • Defence • Taxation • Economic policy • Finance policy • Relations with Europe • Social security • Broadcasting control

SUMMARY

It would be wrong to suggest that Welsh devolution is on a par with the process taking place in Scotland. The fact that the Welsh political system will not be able to pass primary legislation and will have no powers over taxation renders it relatively weak. Laws and taxes are, after all, two of the most fundamental functions of government. Nevertheless, it is an important step.

Welsh devolution is a serious attempt to improve democratic control over the way in which public spending is distributed. It transfers to the region the ability to influence and improve the government of Wales in ways which are approved by those living in Wales, rather than by representatives from all over the United Kingdom in the form of the Westminster Parliament. It may also be that pressure groups operating in the forum of Welsh politics will begin to concentrate their efforts on the Assembly and so have a more direct influence. It may also be that the democratic control of quangos will be strengthened.

It also represents a significant decentralisation of important powers from London to Wales. Large quantities of public funds will be handled in Cardiff. The appointment of key officials in both government and quangos will fall into the hands of Welsh rather than English politicians.

Whether devolution will lead to a stronger sense of Welsh identity remains to be seen. This is certainly the hope of Plaid Cymru who have now adopted full independence, or at least a federal arrangement, as the centrepiece of their policy. It is equally uncertain whether there will be important economic effects. It may well depend upon the attitude of the EU to the new Wales as to how successfully it will be able to promote further development.

THE FUTURE OF NORTHERN IRELAND

It is far beyond a book of this size to tackle the immense issue which has come to be known as the Northern Ireland problem. We must, therefore, limit our discussion to the various options for a new relationship between the province and the rest of the United Kingdom (or the Republic of Ireland for that matter) which might emerge in the future.

The most extreme solution is, of course, that the island of Ireland be re-united as a single sovereign state. To say the least, this remains a distant prospect for the foreseeable future. The Downing Street Declaration of 1993 stated that:

"The British Government agree that it is for the people of the island of Ireland alone, by agreement between the two parts respectively, to exercise their right of self-determination on the basis of consent, freely and concurrently given, North and South, to bring about a united Ireland."

Downing Street Declaration, *December 15, 1993*

The notion that there should be a majority of support in Northern Ireland for unification remains unthinkable as things stand. It might even be the case that the people of the Republic no longer wish to see the North attached to their state. Eire (the Republic of Ireland) has grown in prosperity during the 1990s, largely with the help of the EU, so that acquisition of the six counties in the North is now a less appealing economic opportunity.

We will, therefore, reject this solution as merely an idealistic dream at this stage. Before we consider alternatives, it is important to understand the nature of the two main political movements in Ulster.

UNIONISM AND REPUBLICANISM

The Ulster Unionists, virtually all from the Protestant tradition and represented by a number of political parties, have formed the majority community since partition in 1921. But they are not merely a religious or a political movement. They are one of the most distinctive cultural groupings in the British Isles. This is especially noticeable when it is represented by the clan-like **Orange Lodge**, an organisation which exists largely to keep traditional Ulster Protestant culture alive.

They are fiercely loyal to the British Crown and to the maintenance of the union with the United Kingdom. This is not to say they are committed to support for the British *government*. Indeed, for much of their history they have found themselves in conflict with London government. They are certainly not poodles to British rule. They are a determinedly independent people, intensely proud of their 300 year history, their religion and their own version of Irish culture. Until 1972 they dominated devolved government in Belfast and much of the local government in the province.

With its own Parliament (Stormont) and government led by a prime minister, Northern Ireland enjoyed 50 years of semi-independence, though still not legal sovereignty. These government institutions were completely controlled by unionists, and the Unionist Party, which was unified and closely allied to the English Conservatives, always provided the Prime Minister. Their cause was traditionally supported by the Conservatives, whose full title used to be the Conservative and Unionist Party.

The Ulster unionist culture is difficult to summarise. It is an indefinable combination of English, Irish and Scottish traditions. To some extent it is defensive in character. Although they are now a majority in the province, the Protestant community has spent most of its history as a minority on the island as a whole. Feeling beleaguered in a predominantly Catholic, Gaelic society, it is hardly surprising that they celebrate past military victories which have preserved their position in the North.

The republicans are mainly, though not exclusively, Catholic. They have been a minority since 1921. At that time they had opposed the partition of Ireland and many still vehemently campaign for reunification. Religion is not the only factor which unites them. The community is predominantly working class and has complained for many years of systematic discrimination by the unionist-dominated government, police, legal system, industry and education system.

They feel a closer allegiance to Dublin than to London. As Catholics, the majority also express some religious attachment to the authority of the Pope. Their culture is strongly Irish, anti-English and anti-Protestant. It is difficult to assess the extent to which the Catholic community is republican in its sentiments. Most of them support the Social Democratic Labour Party which is mildly Irish nationalist in its outlook and is mainly concerned with improving the economic prosperity of the poorer Catholic elements of the community. The more radical elements of the minority support Sinn Fein, which is overtly republican.

Lest we might imagine that all the people of Northern Ireland take up extreme political views, we must stress that the middle classes are more moderate in their outlook and prefer to avoid the more radical politics of unionism and republicanism.

THE OPTIONS

Leaving aside the possibility of Irish unification which we have rejected for reasons described above, and the status quo (direct rule), there are a number of possible alternatives for the government of Northern Ireland.

Federalism

A **federal** settlement would grant a good deal of legal sovereignty to an Ulster parliament and government. This would satisfy the demands of both communities for independence from London government, which is normally unpopular. This would be a complete innovation in British regional government. Sovereignty has never been relinquished, so a federal settlement would represent an admission that the social and economic problems of Northern Ireland cannot be solved within the context of the United Kingdom. Nevertheless, under such a system, government in London would retain the right to control the security situation there if necessary.

Devolution

Devolution would return the province to its status before 1972, in an arrangement similar to that which is being installed in Scotland. Were either of these two forms of regional government, devolution or federalism, to be introduced, a proportional system of election and government formation would be essential. The problems which emerged in 1968 and have continued ever since were largely caused by the long-term dominance which the unionists were able to exert over a political system. It is therefore essential that each section of the community should be guaranteed representation in the legislature, in government and on other public bodies. This was recognised when elections for local government and the European Parliament were organised into the STV system.

Joint sovereignty

The most innovatory idea involves some kind of joint sovereignty between Britain and Ireland. There is already some cooperation between the two governments on security matters and cross-border issues, but this more radical proposal implies that a devolved Northern Ireland government would deal with domestic issues such as education, health, social services, housing and local government. Issues concerning internal and external security, legal matters, policing and economic regeneration, however, would be controlled by some kind of joint authority. The nature of such a dual government would be problematic, but the most likely arrangement would be a number of nominated ministers from

London and Dublin. The attraction of dual sovereignty is that it might satisfy the demands of both communities to maintain links with British or Irish government, but would also provide autonomous domestic government and so satisfy the desire of Ulster people for greater independence.

Whatever the future of Northern Ireland, any new governmental arrangements will need to be established with great imagination and will need enormous political will if they are to be successful.

REGIONAL GOVERNMENT FOR ENGLAND?

THE GROWTH OF REGIONAL ADMINISTRATION

The issue of establishing regional government in England is back on the political agenda. However, it has never really been absent since interest emerged in the 1960s. The reality is that there has been extensive regional government for over 30 years. What is being discussed at the end of the century is the possibility of adding *democratic* institutions, in the form of *elected* assemblies or councils. The machinery of regional administration is already in place. This has taken various forms:

- The National Health Service is divided into regional authorities. They are charged with the task of distributing public funds to various smaller health authorities and to other health spending projects.
- After the abolition in 1985 of the GLC and six other metropolitan authorities in England's great conurbations, new regional authorities were set up to oversee the work of the police in these areas. Parallel bodies were set up for the other emergency services, public transport planning and waste management. There are also other large police authorities which transcend local government boundaries, such as the Thames Valley.
- Many quangos are divided on a regional basis. Examples include regional arts councils, sports councils and divisions of the Environment Agency.
- In 1994, ten Integrated Regional Offices were set up, staffed by civil servants. These bodies administer funds under the control of central government departments, notably Transport, Trade and Industry, Employment and Environment.
- Since the EU now makes funds available for regional development through its Committee of the Regions, local authorities have been forced to group together into regional bodies in order to compete for these funds.

So the debate is less about the establishment of regional government and more about how to make the existing system more effective and more democratic.

The case for English regional devolution

The principal thrust of policy in both the Labour and the Liberal Democrat parties is that there needs to be more democratic control and accountability in the regions. However, there also needs to be rationalisation of the system. The detailed case is as follows:

- There is now a great proliferation of regional bodies which are not elected and are insufficiently accountable for their actions.
- Government has become too centralised. Increased regionalism will reduce the power of central government and so enhance democracy.
- The principle of subsidiarity should be followed. This suggests that government should always be carried out on the smallest scale which is reasonable. This enables people to control and participate in government to a greater degree. Regionalisation will transfer many responsibilities from London to smaller units of government throughout England.
- There is now an incoherent and confusing variety of public bodies dealing with regional affairs. There is a need to rationalise and coordinate their work by bringing them all together into single regional administrations.
- There are sufficient disparities in the culture, economic structure, social characteristics and problems in the regions to warrant some degree of separate government.
- There are some aspects of economic development and planning which must be organised on a regional basis if they are to reap the benefits of efficiency. In short, if left to local government, the small-scale nature of the operation would be detrimental. This is especially true of industrial regeneration, public transport, environmental protection and countryside development.

The case against regional devolution

The Conservative Party remains firmly opposed to such proposals, as do some elements in the Labour Party. They have a number of compelling objections:

- It may lead to the break up of Britain. This is similar to their opposition to devolution in Scotland and Wales. Having set up centrifugal political forces, it may prove difficult to control them.
- Adding another layer of government will be expensive, lead to too much bureaucracy and confusion among the public, and may cause a loss of efficiency. Thus, far from limiting government, it would create too much government.
- Opponents deny that there are significant social, economic and cultural differences in various parts of England. Regionalism would deny the essential unity of the country.
- It would lead to a widening of economic differences between the regions. With unified government it is possible to transfer resources from one region to another in order to promote national equality. Less of this process will occur under a regional system so that the richer regions may continue to prosper, while poorer regions decline further.

PROSPECTS UNDER LABOUR

The Labour Party is less certain about its attitude to English regional government than it has been to equivalent plans in Scotland or Wales. However, both Home Secretary Jack Straw and Deputy Leader John Prescott remain committed to exploring the possibility further.

The centrepiece of the proposals is the confirmation of the ten Integrated Regional Offices (IROs), with expanded responsibilities to cover many of the other regional bodies which exist and confuse the picture. These would come under the direct democratic control of regional associations made up of representatives from local authorities within the region.

This would remain under only indirect control. However, if the system appears to be working, and if it proves popular with the public, the associations would be replaced by directly elected regional assemblies. This would create devolution very much along the lines of the system to be introduced in Wales after 2000.

STUDY GUIDES

Revision Hints

The advantages and disadvantages of devolution and regional government should be clearly noted. Most questions on the subject will require such an analysis.

The reasons behind the drive for devolution in Scotland and Wales should be listed, with special attention paid to the key events and stages in he development of the issue. In addition, distinctions between the circumstances of Scotland, Wales and Northern Ireland should be made.

Clearly it is essential that you should have a clear picture of how devolution actually works in constitutional terms, how power has divided and what is the new relationship between the devolved governments and central government in London.

The role, both positive and negative, of quangos must be noted. Identify their various roles and how this would be affected by devolution.

The most likely question to be posed is how devolution proposals came about. This will apply to English regions in addition to the three national areas. Answers should be sensitive to the attitudes of the parties and other groups to devolution as well as expressing the reservations which opponents had.

Assessments of devolution and regional government must clearly show what the advantages are, as well as the problems which can arise from the process. In this regard, the political and economic consequences should be specifically identified.

Questions about the future of Northern Ireland are especially difficult because the province does not conform to the characteristics of Scotland, Wales and England. Special attention needs to be paid to the unique cultural factors there.

In all cases, the important role of quangos should be referred to. They are both agents of regional government, and one of the reasons why there have been calls for devolution which might improve democracy. Quangos are often seen as undemocratic, so devolution may be an antidote to their effects.

Practice Questions

1 a Why has devolution become an important issue in Scotland and Wales in the 1990s?
   b Will the 1997 proposals answer the demands for devolution adequately?
2 Should devolution be extended to the English regions?
3 a Do you believe that devolution will lead to the break up of the United Kingdom?
   b Can a case be made for such a break up?
4 Are devolution or federalism potential answers to the Northern Ireland problem?

8

CONCLUSIONS AND SUMMARY

WHAT ARE THE dominant themes which we should pick out from this vast subject? It is especially difficult to answer this question at the end of the millennium, as so much radical change is under way. But we must make an attempt and at least we can be helped by some alliteration. The trends and processes described in the book may be distilled down to three 'Ds':

- Devolution
- Decentralisation
- Democratisation

These three ideas overlap considerably, of course, but we can pick out their own distinctive characteristics.

DEVOLUTION

GOVERNMENT BY CONSENT

The devolution movement recognises two basic principles. First, that the doctrine of government by consent must be reconfirmed in the United Kingdom. This concept which has been asserted and reasserted in such documents as Woodrow Wilson's 14 principles established after the First World War, the United Nations Declaration and various treaties of the EU. But why did we need to test it in Britain in 1997?

The answer is that there were growing indications that the Scots and the Welsh did wish to withdraw their consent to be governed by current arrangements. Support for nationalist parties, the total rejection of the unionist Conservative

Party and their enthusiastic embrace of the proposals unveiled in Labour's 1997 election manifesto were the main manifestations. But in addition, more sensitive politicians had recognised the signs long before 1997.

The solution to this suspicion had to be to ask the Scots and the Welsh whether they wanted a new constitutional settlement. It is likely that in the near future the people of London, of Northern Ireland and perhaps of the English regions will be given a similar opportunity.

SELF-DETERMINATION

This doctrine suggests that, if a people have recognisably separate, distinctive culture, they have the right to determine their own system of government and should have the power to make important decisions which will affect them as a whole.

The question which had to be asked in the 1990s was whether the Scots and the Welsh fulfilled the necessary criteria. If devolution is seriously to be considered for the English regions, it will have to be addressed again. The distinctive characteristics must not be superficial; this will lead to disappointment and resentment. But if there are fundamental enough differences, the idea of self-determination can take firm hold.

DECENTRALISATION

The last quarter of the twentieth century saw a general drift towards the centralisation of powers in Britain. This process can be detailed as follows:

- The introduction of direct rule in Northern Ireland in 1972.
- The transfer of many local government responsibilities either to ministers or to quangos which were effectively controlled by those same ministers. These have included urban regeneration, transport, housing and planning.
- The ever-tightening control exercised by the Treasury over the finance of public services. Apart from the well documented loss of financial independence of local government, there has also been increasing discipline in such areas as the health service, the police, the Welsh and Scottish Offices and the many public expenditure quangos which now flourish.
- The abolition of the seven metropolitan authorities in 1986 took away a whole level of local government from many millions of people.

This trend is being reversed, especially after the 1997 Election. Apart from devolution as described above, there are proposals for more regional government, possibly with elected regional assemblies, for increased autonomy for local government and transfers of many powers from quangos back to local regional government. Optimistic though it may seem, there is even a possibility that Northern Ireland will once again be able to govern itself.

DEMOCRATISATION

The loss of local autonomy, the takeover of responsibilities from elected authorities to unelected quangos, the continuing problems of local government accountability as identified by Widdicombe, and the loss of many vehicles for local opinion, have all led to fears that British democracy is in serious decline. The problem is writ large in Northern Ireland where district authorities are under tight control from the Northern Ireland Office, and the lower levels of local government have scarcely more independence than English parish councils.

Clearly, if regional and local government can be revitalised, democracy will benefit. However, there is more to reform than that. The introduction of greater sensitivity to public opinion of local authorities and the use of elected, accountable mayors will go some way to reverse the trend. It is devolution, with its powerful elected assemblies, however, which will result in most progress. The new Scottish and Welsh executives will provide more democratic control over quangos and other public bodies. A similar arrangement in Northern Ireland will have similar effect.

The progress of democratisation may prove to be short-lived. The reforming zeal of the Labour government which won in 1997 may not be enduring. The realities of power and its problems may well force the government to rein back its proposals to transfer large amounts of power back to the people. But for those who welcome the new atmosphere, there is room for optimism.

GLOSSARY

Audit Commission Body which checks the efficiency and effectiveness of public organisations such as local authorities.

Barnett Formula A scheme to bring public expenditure in Scotland down to the same level as the rest of the UK.

Best Value A principle that local government services should be provided both as well and as cheaply as possible.

Challenge Funding Funds for which local authorities can compete for capital spending projects.

Charge capping Power exercised by ministers to limit increases in local taxation.

Citizens' Charter A principle whereby public bodies should be accountable to the public for the quality of their performance.

Community Charge See under Poll Tax.

Community Councils Third tier authorities in Scotland.

Compulsory Competitive Tendering Requirement that local authorities offer various service provisions out to private tender.

Corporatism A style of politics where important interest groups are incorporated formally into the governing process.

Council Tax Local property tax used after 1992.

Devolution The process of transferring large amounts of power, but not sovereignty, to a region.

Direct Democracy A system where the people directly make decisions without use of representatives.

Federalism A system of government where legal sovereignty is divided between central government and defined regions or states.

Gerrymandering The practice of drawing up political boundaries to favour one's own party.

Greater London Council A London-wide authority existing between 1965–86.

Inner London Education Authority An education authority run jointly by 12 inner London boroughs between 1965 and 1990.

Insiders and Outsiders A name for pressure groups devised by Professor Wyn Grant. Insiders have a formal, permanent role in advising government; outsiders do not and so must rely on public pressure.

Joint Boards Bodies which represent several local authorities in the provision of a broad scale service.

Legal Sovereignty The highest authority to make laws which is reserved and cannot be overruled by any superior body.

Local Government Commission Body set up in 1992 to consider new local government structure in England and Wales.

Macrory Report 1972 report on local government in Northern Ireland.

Militant Tendency A leftwing faction of the Labour Party which flourished in local government in the 1980s.

Neo-liberalism 1980s and 90s philosophy that the state should interfere in economic affairs as little as possible.

New Magistracy A term applied to those who fill top positions on major quangos.

Nolan Committee Set up in 1995 to investigate standards in public life.

Orange Lodge An organisation in Northern Ireland dedicated to preserving the culture and traditions of the protestant unionist community there.

Parish Councils Third tier authorities in England and Wales.

Patronage The practice of granting offices and honours to one's supporters in order to gain political power.

Plaid Cymru The Welsh National Party.

Poll Tax Also known as Community Charge. Per capita local tax used between 1989–92.

Precept Portion of tax collected and transferred from one local authority to another on another tier.

Private Finance Initiative A way of funding capital projects through a combination of private and local authority finance.

Public Works Loans Board Central government body which lends money to local authorities for capital spending projects.

Quango Standing for Quasi Autonomous Non (originally National) Organisation. An official body which is appointed and funded by government but which in theory is expected to operate independently of national government and party politics.

Redcliffe-Maude Committee An inquiry into local government structure set up in the 1970s.

Standard Spending Assessment The annual assessment by officials of each local authority's spending needs.

STV Single Transferable Vote. A system of voting in multi-member constituencies. It awards seats in proportion to voting for the parties. It also gives voters a wide choice of candidates.

Subsidiarity The principle that government should be as close to the people (ie, on as small a scale) as possible.

Uniform Business Rate Standard rate of local tax levied on industrial and commercial premises.

Unitary State A state where legal sovereignty is concentrated in central government.

Urban Development Corporations Public bodies set up to organise and finance regeneration of cities.

West Lothian Question The controversy over the right of Scottish MPs to vote on English and Welsh affairs after devolution.

Widdicombe Report The report of a committee into the internal workings of local government.

FURTHER READING

ARTICLES

The first place to start for further reading should be relevant articles in two journals – *Talking Politics* and *Politics Review*. Both contain material by leading authorities in the field, and cover the key elements in the local, regional and devolved government. Recent articles include:

Talking Politics
'The Transformation of the State', M. Burch et al, Winter 1994–5
'Evaluating the Quango State', T. Stott, Winter 1995–6
'Do We Need Regional Government?' G. Stoker et al, Spring 1996
Local Government: Becoming a Backwater or Heading for Renewal? H. Elcock, Autumn 1997

Politics Review
'Change in Local Government', J. Stewart, November 1995
'Standing for Ulster', M. Cunningham and R. Kelly, November 1995
'The Devolution Debate in Scotland', J. Jewell, February 1996
'The Local Government Review', S. Leach, February 1996
'English Regional Government', J. Bradbury, April 1996
'Quangos in British Politics', D. Wilson, September 1996
'Northern Ireland: The Search for Peace and Political Progress', S. Hopkins, April 1997
'More Tory Blues in 1996 Local Elections', C. Rallings and M. Thrasher, September 1996

OTHER PUBLICATIONS

The best guides to devolution and to London government are the official publications on the subjects. These are:

Scotland's Parliament, Cm3658 (HMSO, 1997)
New Leadership for London, Cm3724 (HMSO, 1997)
A Voice for Wales, Cm3718 (HMSO, 1997)

On regional government there is an excellent Fabian Society document:

Devolving Power: The Case for Regional Government, A. Coulsdon.

Also the final report of the Commission for Local Democracy in 1995 entitled *The Rebirth of Local Government* states the case clearly.

BOOKS

There are also a number of useful books for those who need to study the subject in greater depth. These include:

Local Government in the United Kingdom, Wilson and Game (Macmillan, 1994)
A thorough and accessible guide to the subject. It has great detail and is extremely comprehensive.

Local Government in Britain, Tony Byrne (editor) (Penguin, 1994)
This is especially strong in describing the internal workings of local authorities and in discussing the relations between central and local government.

Local Government and Politics in Britain, John Kingdom (Philip Allan, 1991)
Another accessible textbook designed for A level, but thorough enough to be useful for undergraduates.

The Politics of Local Government, Gerry Stoker (Macmillan, 1991)
As the title suggests, especially strong on local politics and the issue of local democracy, written by one of the most respected authorities on the subject.

Devolution, Vernon Bogdanor (Oxford University Press, 1979)
This is a clear explanation of why devolution came to the top of the political agenda in the 1970s.

The Battle for Scotland, Andrew Marr (Penguin, 1995)
A journalist's eye view of politics in Scotland.

INDEX